The Learning Works

# THE BOX

## Creative Projects to Make Using Boxes

Fun Cross-Curriculum Activities!

Grades 3–6

Math Rap CD

Detective Kit

Book Report Float

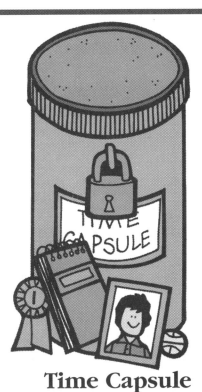

Time Capsule

Written by Ramona Otto and Jocelyn Balaban
Illustrated by Beverly Armstrong

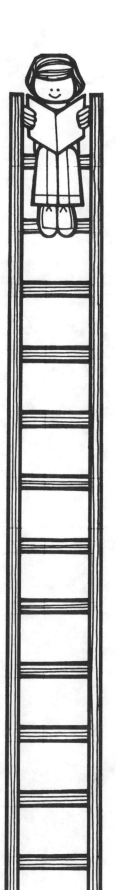

# The Learning Works

*Cover Design and Illustrations:*
 Bev Armstrong

*Editing and Text Design:*
 Clark Editorial & Design

Copyright © 1998
**The Learning Works, Inc.**
Santa Barbara, California 93160

**ISBN: 0-88160-289-2**
**LW 359**

Printed in the United States of America.

# Introduction: To the Teacher

*The Box Book* is a collection of creative activities that will add pizzazz to your academic program in all areas of the curriculum. These activities highlight important skills that will motivate your students in math, reading, science, social studies, and writing. These stimulating projects are created from common boxes and containers such as shoe boxes, cereal boxes, oatmeal boxes, bandage boxes, and cake boxes. Your students' imaginations will soar as they learn new facts and reinforce concepts already learned. Additionally, the completed projects make eye-catching displays for your open houses and back-to-school nights.

3

# Table of Contents

# Table of Contents
## continued

*The Box Book*
© The Learning Works, Inc.

# Table of Contents
## continued

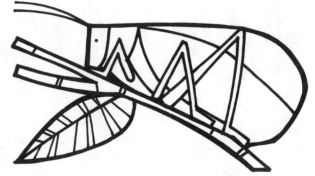

# Capture the Moment: To the Teacher

One way to help students become better writers is to expose them to the works of award-winning authors. Select passages that are appropriate for your class. You may wish to use an overhead projector, or hand out individual copies of the text.

As you share descriptive passages, point out the use of metaphors, similes, personification, and unusual, vocabulary-stretching words. Show how these techniques can be used to make stories interesting and exciting, and encourage your students to incorporate them into their own work.

This Capture-the-Moment Camera is an excellent follow-up project to use with a reading assignment. Made from a butter or margarine box, it holds cards on which a student has written favorite descriptive passages from a book he or she has read. (Adult help is necessary to complete this project, since the use of a sharp craft knife is required.) As a culminating activity, students will create their own "capture-the-moment" scenes as part of a class photo album.

A sample card is shown below. Before beginning this project, you may wish to teach or review the use of quotation marks and the ellipsis as used in quotations.

"In her attic bedroom Margaret Murry, wrapped in an old patchwork quilt . . . watched the trees tossing in the frenzied lashing of the wind. Behind the trees, clouds scudded frantically across the sky. Every few moments the moon ripped through them, creating wraith-like shadows that raced along the ground."

—from *A Wrinkle in Time* by Madeleine L'Engle

*The Box Book*
© The Learning Works, Inc.

# Capture the Moment

Authors capture moments in time by describing scenes and events so vividly that they come to life in the reader's imagination. Like snapshots, these word pictures can be enjoyed again and again.

Follow the directions below to build this butter-box "camera." Then browse through a book you have recently read and select some of your favorite descriptive passages. Copy these word pictures on Quotation Cards, and store the cards in your camera.

## What You Need

one-pound butter or margarine box
masking tape
craft knife
Capture-the-Moment Camera Patterns (pages 9–10)
Quotation Card Patterns (page 11)
markers or crayons
scissors
glue
pen or pencil
Photo Album Page (page 12)

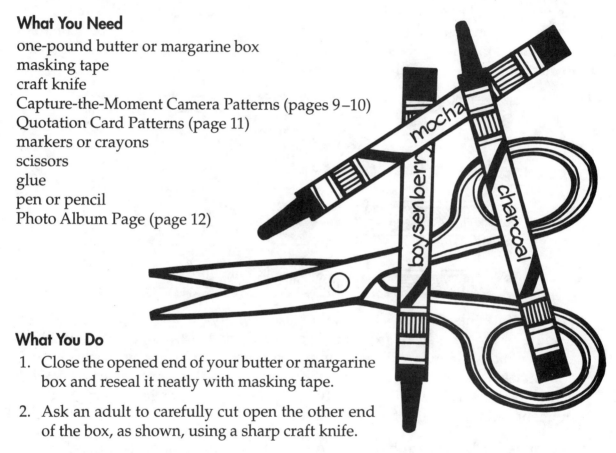

## What You Do

1.  Close the opened end of your butter or margarine box and reseal it neatly with masking tape.

2.  Ask an adult to carefully cut open the other end of the box, as shown, using a sharp craft knife.

3.  Now prepare your camera pattern pieces (pages 9 and 10) according to the directions provided.

4.  Glue the front/top/side piece to the box as shown, so its side flap fits over the flap of your box. This end of the box must be able to open and close.

5.  Glue the back pattern piece to the box.

6.  Store your Quotation Cards inside the camera.

7.  Now it's time for you to be the author. Write your own "capture-the-moment" scene on the Photo Album Page (page 12). Illustrate the scene in the "photo." Put your page with those of your classmates to create a class photo album.

# Capture-the-Moment Camera Pattern

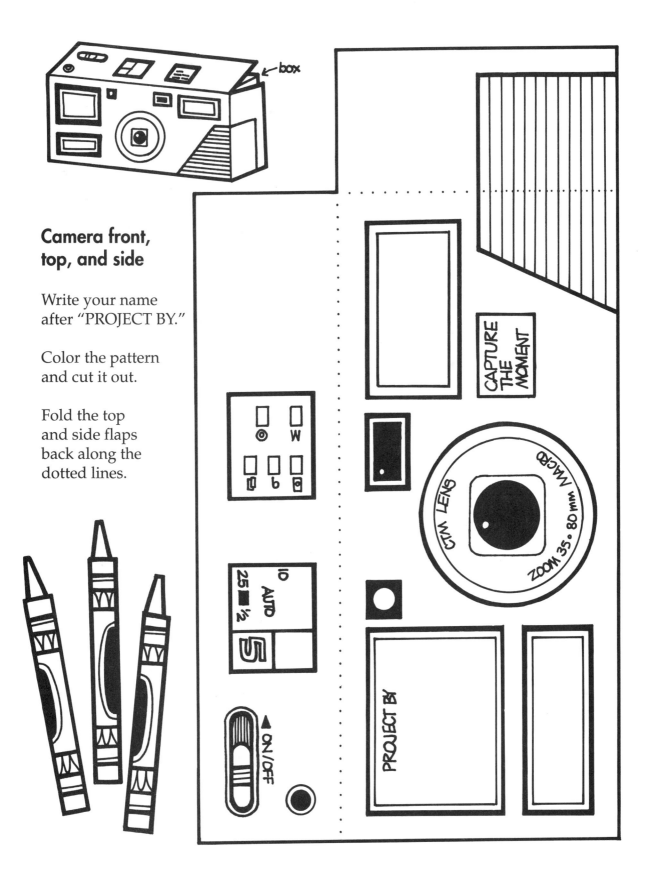

**Camera front, top, and side**

Write your name after "PROJECT BY."

Color the pattern and cut it out.

Fold the top and side flaps back along the dotted lines.

CAPTURE THE MOMENT

CTM LENS

ZOOM 35 • 80 mm MACRO

AUTO
10
25
½
5

ON/OFF

PROJECT BY

*The Box Book*
© The Learning Works, Inc.

# Capture-the-Moment Camera Pattern

## Camera back and side

Write the title and author
of your book on the lines.

Color the pattern and cut it out.

Fold the side flap back along
the dotted line.

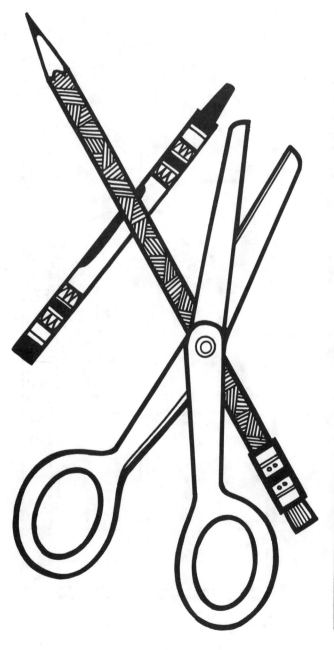

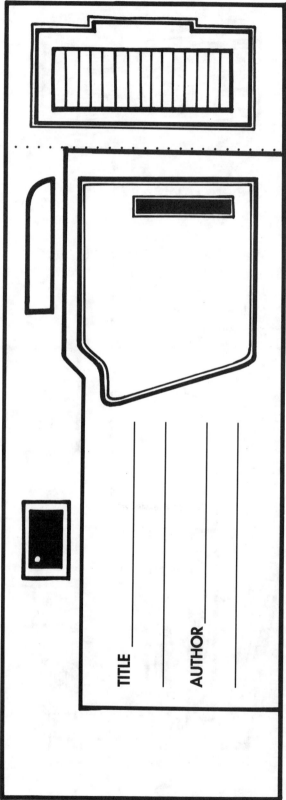

TITLE

AUTHOR

# Quotation Card Patterns

Duplicate as needed.

**Quote:** _____

_____

_____

_____

_____

_____

**Page** _____

**Quote:** _____

_____

_____

_____

_____

_____

**Page** _____

**Quote:** _____

_____

_____

_____

_____

_____

**Page** _____

*The Box Book*
© The Learning Works, Inc.

_____'s

# Photo Album Page

# Hero-O Cereal: To the Teacher

In this project, each student gets to invent a new cereal and then picture himself or herself on the box! Also included in the box design are a story of the student's real or imaginary exploits and accomplishments, and descriptions of the cereal and prize inside.

After completing the cereal boxes, students will create television commercials for their new products. Writing scripts for these advertisements is an opportunity for learning or reviewing play-writing techniques—how speaking parts are set up, how colons are used, and how parentheses are used to show directions.

**Example:**

DOG: It's tough being a dog. (He sighs and shakes his head.) I have to watch my owner chowing down on crunchy Hero-O Cereal every morning. My dog food just sits in my bowl getting soggy.

Your students will enjoy the opportunity to perform their commercials in front of their peers. Consider videotaping the presentation!

*The Box Book*
© The Learning Works, Inc.

# Hero-O Cereal

Cereal boxes often feature pictures and stories of people who excel in sports or other areas. Imagine a cereal box honoring *you*, with your face on the front and a story about great things you have done (real or make-believe) on the back. Now design and create that box. Let the world know what a hero you are!

## What You Need

cereal box
scratch paper at least as big as the front of your box
construction paper in various colors
Cereal Box Lettering Patterns (page 17)
pencil
ruler
scissors
tape or glue
crayons or markers
photo of yourself (optional)
Hero-O Cereal Commercial Script and Picture (pages 18–19),
    one or more copies of each

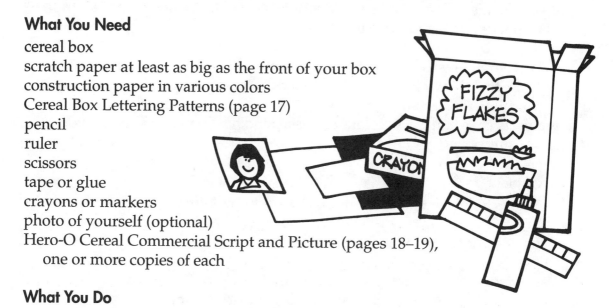

## What You Do

1.  Cut out two pieces of scratch paper the size of the front of your cereal box, and two pieces the size of its side. You can do this by putting the box on a piece of paper, drawing around it, and cutting out the shapes you have drawn.

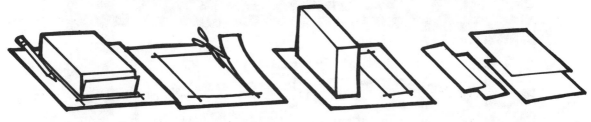

2.  Now think about the story that will go on the back of the box. Is there something you have done (such as helping others, getting good grades, or being a valuable player on your soccer team) that you want to tell about, or would you rather make up an imaginary story about your life as a superhero? Write a rough draft of your story on one of the larger pieces of scratch paper. You may wish to leave space for drawings or a border.

3.  Cut a piece of construction paper the size of the back of your box. Carefully copy your story onto it. Use crayons and markers to add color. Then tape or glue your story to the back of your cereal box.

# Hero-O Cereal
## continued

4. Prizes make cereal more fun! Design a prize related to your story to feature on one side panel of your box. Draw this prize and write an exciting description of it on the scratch paper you have prepared. After making any needed changes or corrections, copy your work onto a strip of construction paper cut to fit on the side of your box. Add color with crayons or markers, and tape or glue the paper to the box.

5. On the other side panel, describe Hero-O Cereal. What does it look like? How does it taste? What is it made of? What nutrients does it contain? Does it make a sound when milk is added? Plan your design on a piece of scratch paper, then carefully copy it onto construction paper. Color your work and glue or tape it to the side of your box.

6. The design on the front of a cereal box is important, because people often decide whether or not to buy things depending on what the package looks like. Your design will need to include the things listed below.

   • the name "Hero-O Cereal"

   • a photo or drawing of yourself, and a few words telling why you were chosen to appear on the box

   • a brief description of the cereal (examples: honey-sweetened wheat, crunchy chocolate circles)

   • the amount of cereal in the box

   • information about the prize

   Experiment with several designs on scratch paper before creating your final, full-color art on construction paper and attaching it to the box. Use the lettering patterns on page 17 if needed.

*The Box Book*
© The Learning Works, Inc.

# Hero-O Cereal
## continued

7. Now that your box is finished, you can write a commercial to promote your new cereal. There are three parts to this project: writing the script, drawing one or more scenes from the commercial, and presenting the commercial to your class. For your presentation, you can either read the script while displaying the scene(s) you have drawn, or you can actually act out your commercial.

8. When writing your script, consider these things:

   • How much time do you have? (Many commercials are 30 seconds long.)

   • What information do you need to give?

   • What will be the *tone* of your commercial—happy, silly, scary, mysterious, exciting?

   • What will be the *setting*—kitchen, science lab, circus, football field, Mars?

   • What *character(s)* will be in the commercial—clown, gymnast, bear, race car driver, baby, parrot, cowboy?

   Practice writing scripts on scratch paper. When your script is ready, copy it onto the form on page 18. Use as many pages as you need.

9. Use scratch paper to draw one or more scenes from your commercial. (When drawing a scene from your commercial, think about things that will make people want to watch the whole commercial and then buy the cereal.) Use the form on page 19 to create your final drawing. (If you are drawing more than one scene, ask your teacher for additional copies.)

10. When presenting your commercial, you may wish to use masks or costumes, puppets, magic tricks, and/or sound effects. Have fun!

# Cereal Box Lettering Patterns

HERO-O CEREAL

Hero-o Cereal

HERO-O CEREAL

HERO-O CEREAL

HERO-O CEREAL

HERO-O CEREAL

HERO-O CEREAL

HERO-O CEREAL

HERO-O CEREAL

*The Box Book*
© The Learning Works, Inc.

# Hero-O Cereal Commercial Script

Name _____

Power    Volume    Channel

# Hero-O Cereal Commercial Picture

Name _____

Power

Volume  − +

Channel  ◄ ►

*The Box Book*
© The Learning Works, Inc.

# Oatmeal Box Time Capsule:
# To the Teacher

Pick a week at the beginning of the school year or the new semester to begin this project. To make the time capsules, each student will fill an empty oatmeal box with a variety of things including a handwriting sample, a list of goals, photos or drawings, and five personal items the student has selected. Before sealing the capsules, give the students a chance to describe the items they have selected and to explain why they chose to include them. This provides a chance for each student to speak before the class and is an ideal way for kids to get to know each other better. Pack the completed time capsules in a large box and give the box to your school maintenance engineer to store in a safe place until the end of the school year. Your students will enjoy browsing through their time capsules, comparing handwriting samples, and taking their capsules home as keepsakes.

# Oatmeal Box Time Capsule

Get ready to pack a "glimpse of you" into a time capsule to put away and then retrieve at the end of the school year. You'll have fun seeing how much you've grown and changed during the year.

**What You Need**

empty oatmeal box (18-ounce size)
scissors
pencil
markers
glue
letter to parents (page 22)
Time Capsule Label (page 23)
Time Capsule activities (pages 24–32)
Time Capsule Lock (page 33)
five personal items
photo or drawing of yourself
photo or drawing of your family

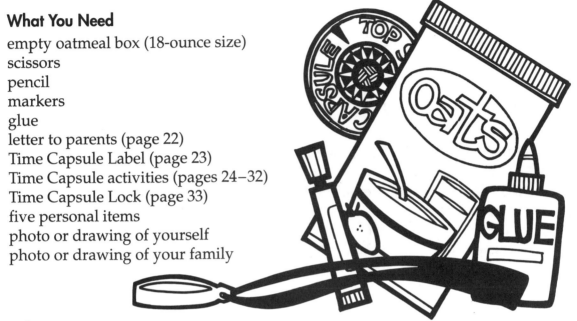

**What You Do**

1. Take the letter home to your parents to read.

2. Bring an empty oatmeal box to class.

3. Fill out the Time Capsule Label on page 23. Color and decorate your label. Cut it out and glue it to your box.

4. Complete the Handwriting Sample on page 24 in your neatest writing. When the Time Capsules are opened at the end of the school year, you'll be asked to complete another sample of your handwriting and compare the two.

5. Complete the remaining Time Capsule activities on pages 25–32.

6. Select five small items that represent you to place in your Time Capsule—for example, a drawing of the cover of your favorite book, a sample baseball card from a collection, or a picture of your dog.

7. Be prepared to explain to your classmates why you selected these items for your Time Capsule.

8. Put all of your items and completed activity sheets in the Time Capsule.

9. Color the Time Capsule Lock (page 33). Cut it out and glue it to the lid of your Time Capsule.

# A Letter to Parents

Dear Parent,

A time capsule is like a scrapbook. Putting a time capsule together is fun—and it's exciting for the kids to browse through the contents of their time capsules at the end of the school year.

During class time this week, our students will be preparing personal time capsules and completing a series of fun and creative activities. These activities will help orient students to a new academic setting and help them feel more secure during the get-acquainted process of a new school year.

Much of the homework time this week will be devoted to preparing items to include in the time capsules. We have asked each student to select five items that represent him or her at the present time. Ideas include a tape of your child reading a story at his or her current reading level, a souvenir from a recent vacation, an item that represents a hobby or special interest, a drawing or craft made by your child, or the hardest math problem your child can do. Please help your child select five items to bring to school on Friday. Students will be given an opportunity to share their choices with classmates. Your child will also need an empty oatmeal box (18-ounce size) in which to store his or her items.

We will "bury" our time capsules in a safe place until the last week of school, when they will be opened.

Thank you for your assistance with this project.

Sincerely,

**TIME CAPSULE**

PROPERTY OF

DATE SEALED:

DO NOT OPEN UNTIL:

*The Box Book*
© The Learning Works, Inc.

# Handwriting Sample

Copy this paragraph in your best handwriting
on the "Before" form provided below.

**My name is (first name) (last name). I attend (school name).
I am (        ) years old and I am in the (        ) grade. My
teacher's name is (                    ).**

Date _____

**Before**

_____
_____
_____
_____
_____
_____

Date _____

**After**

_____
_____
_____
_____
_____
_____

Name _____

# Fascinating Facts About Me

my birthday _____

city where I was born _____

members of my family _____

_____

pets that belong to my family _____

my best friends _____

hobbies I enjoy _____

things I collect _____

the best book I ever read _____

lessons I have taken _____

my favorite foods _____

places I have lived _____

the last movie I saw _____

my favorite type of music _____

sports or games I enjoy playing _____

a place I like to vacation _____

an interesting fact about me _____

_____

*The Box Book*
© The Learning Works, Inc.

# Presenting Me

Draw a picture of yourself, or paste a recent photograph
of yourself in the space below.

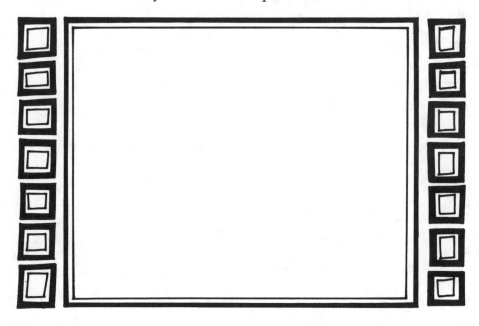

height _____ feet _____ inches

weight _____ pounds

age _____ years _____ months _____ days

length and color of my hair _____

number of freckles that I have _____

number of teeth that I have _____

wrist size in inches _____

ankle size in inches _____

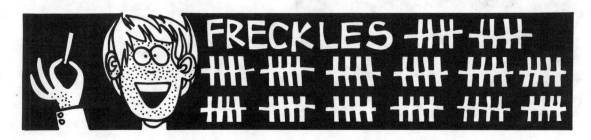

Name _____

# A Family Photo

Draw a picture of your family, or paste a
recent family photograph in the space below.

## A Who's Who of My Family

Write a brief sentence about each family member in your photograph.

_____

_____

_____

_____

_____

_____

_____

Name _____

# Inventory Sheet

List the five items you are putting in the Time Capsule, and explain why you are including them.

1. _____

_____

_____

2. _____

_____

_____

3. _____

_____

_____

4. _____

_____

_____

5. _____

_____

_____

# Predictions for the Future

On a separate piece of paper, write a paragraph describing what your life and the world around you might be like in the year 2025. Think about the following: careers, family life, living conditions, transportation, clothing and hair styles, and entertainment. Revise and edit your work. Write your final draft below.

_____
_____
_____
_____
_____
_____
_____
_____
_____
_____
_____
_____
_____
_____

# Headline Happenings

If you were to read only the headlines of a major newspaper for a year, you would have a good summary of all the major events that took place in that year. Imagine what newspaper headlines might be in the year 2025. Have space aliens landed? Do cars fly? For each category listed below, write a headline that might appear in a newspaper in the year 2025.

international news _____

national news _____

state news _____

local news _____

sports _____

fashion _____

business _____

entertainment _____

weather _____

**Just for Fun**

Create a comic strip of the future.

Name _____

# Goals for the Year

For each heading, write a goal for the school year.

something new I would like to try _____

number of books I would like to read _____

someone in class I would like to get to know better_____

a bad habit I would like to get rid of_____

a skill I would like to improve in _____

a subject I would like to improve in _____

a hobby I would like to explore _____

a musical, artistic, or athletic goal I would like to achieve _____

31

*The Box Book*
© The Learning Works, Inc.

Name _____

# Goals for the Year Checklist

When you open your Time Capsule at the end of the school year, check to see how well you have done in meeting your goals.

Something new I tried this year is _____ .

This year I read _____ books.

I got to know _____ better this year.

_____ is a bad habit I got rid of this year.

_____ is a skill I improved in.

_____ is a subject I improved in.

This year, I explored _____ as a hobby.

A musical, artistic, or athletic goal I pursued this year is _____ .

How many of the goals you set at the beginning of the year did you achieve? _____

# Time Capsule Lock

# Reading Takes the Cake:
# To the Teacher

Your students will "eat up" this "sweet" book report project with its special emphasis on character development and analysis. You can use this activity with a class novel, or ask students to select fiction books to read independently. Use the approval form on page 37 to check the suitability of each student's individual selection. Show your students a completed sample of the "Reading Takes the Cake" box before beginning this project. It will help them visualize and plan their projects.

If I could spend an afternoon with Amy, I'd like to ride around the farm with her on the ponies, Copper and Cocoa. I'd bring some brownies I had made for us to eat. Later I would show Amy how I draw horses, and she could show me her rock collection.

# Reading Takes the Cake

Read a fiction book of your choice, and then "stir" up all your talents to put the "icing" on the cake box you create!

## What You Need

fiction book
Book Report Approval Form (page 37)
Box Cover (page 38)
cake box
pencil or pen
markers
scissors
glue
activity sheets (pages 39–44)
construction paper (9" x 12" in a variety of colors, including skin tones)
yarn for faces (12" lengths in hair colors)
Sketch Your Favorite Character (page 45)
Favorite Character Collage (page 46)
Diorama Diagrams (page 47)
oaktag (9" x 10")

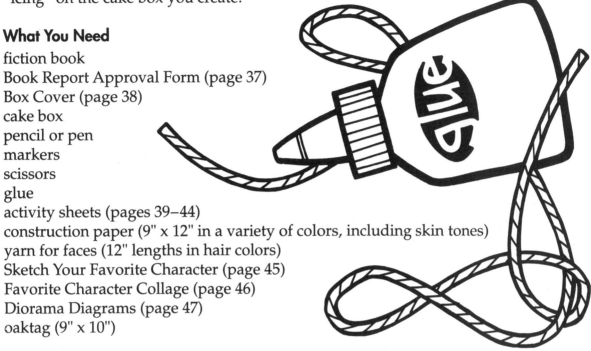

## What You Do

1. Check out a fiction book from the school library or your public library.

2. Fill out the Book Report Approval Form (page 37) and have your teacher sign it.

3. Fill out the information on the Box Cover (page 38). Color the Box Cover, cut it out, and glue it to the top of your cake box.

*The Box Book*
© The Learning Works, Inc.

# Reading Takes the Cake
## continued

4. Fill in the cake-piece activity sheets on pages 39–44. Make sure that they are done in your best handwriting. Cut out the pieces.

5. Put the cake box together as your teacher directs. Glue the cake pieces to the sides of your cake box, as shown on page 47.

6. Using scratch paper, sketch the face of your favorite character from the book.

7. Using your sketch as your guide, create a collage of your favorite character's face. Follow the directions on page 46.

8. On a separate piece of paper, draw a rough-draft sketch of your favorite part of the book. This will help you visualize the scene you'll create for your diorama.

9. Now use your sketch to help you build a diorama out of oaktag. Be sure to include a tab on each piece so you can attach it to the cake box as shown. Color and cut out your pieces, and glue them to the inside of the cake box. (See the diagrams on page 47.)

10. Enjoy sharing your "Reading Takes the Cake" diorama with your classmates.

# Book Report Approval Form

Student's name _____

Title of book _____

Author _____

Illustrator _____

Type of book _____


Approved _____

(teacher's signature)

37

**READING TAKES THE CAKE**

**TITLE** _____

**AUTHOR** _____

**ILLUSTRATOR** _____

**PROJECT BY** _____

# Story Setting

Briefly describe the setting of the story.

## Things to Think About

- Where does the story take place (city, state, country, etc.)?
- What buildings are important in the story?
- During what year and season does the story take place?
- What does the setting's landscape look like?

INDIA·TEXAS·PADUCAH
VERMONT·THE ANDES
MUD LICK·UTAH·AFRICA

*The Box Book*
© The Learning Works, Inc.

# Character's Personality

Describe your favorite character's personality.

**Things to Think About**

- Find a sentence in the book that describes your favorite character's personality.

- Describe how he or she gets along with other people.

- What one word would you use to describe your favorite character?

- What makes your character special?

- Would you enjoy being this character's friend? Why or why not?

- Does your favorite character remind you of someone you know?

FRIENDLY·LAZY·BRAVE·HELPFUL
CURIOUS·KIND·FUNNY·SNEAKY

# Character's Appearance

Write a brief description of your favorite character's appearance.

**Things to Think About**

- How old is your favorite character?

- Is your favorite character male or female?

- What is the character's height, eye color, and hair color?

- Does the character wear glasses?

- Describe any special physical characteristics, such as freckles, long legs, or a muscular build.

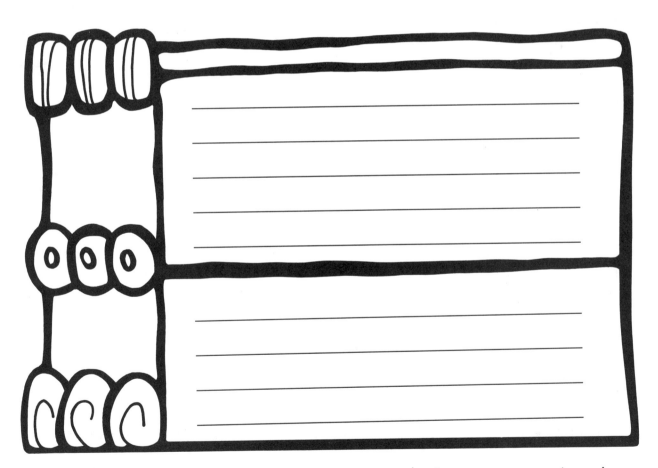

big brown eyes · awkward · long pigtails
huge smile · braces · tall · skinned knees

# Important Events

Choose five of the most important story events and list them in chronological order.

**Things to Think About**

- How did the story begin?

- What problems needed to be solved in the story?

- What exciting events lead to the turning point in the story?

- How did the story end?

1. Ramona starts going to Kindergarten.
2. Ramona keeps getting in trouble.
3. Miss Binney is missing.
4. Ramona is sent home from school.
5. Ramona gets Miss Binney's letter.

# Character Changes

What changes does your character go through in the story?
Describe one important change and the events that caused it.

**Things to Think About**

- In the story, did your character change in age or appearance?

- What things did he or she learn?

- Did his or her behavior change? If so, in what ways?

MONSTER TODDLER
silly seven·year·old
responsible teenager

# My Character and Me

If you were to spend an afternoon with your character,
what would you choose for an activity and why?

**Things to Think About**

- What personality traits does the character have that appeal to you? Why?

- What interests or hobbies do you and this character share?

- What could you teach your character? What could your character teach you?

SKATEBOARDING·CHESS
PETS·MODEL TRAINS
ASTRONOMY·INSECTS

# Sketch Your Favorite Character

Create a portrait of your favorite character to fit inside the lid of your cake box. Sketch your character's face in the space below. The head should be at least six inches tall. You will use this drawing as a pattern for making a collage.

Think about your character's face and hair. Does he or she wear a hat, glasses, or jewelry? Use passages from the book to help you draw your character as accurately as possible.

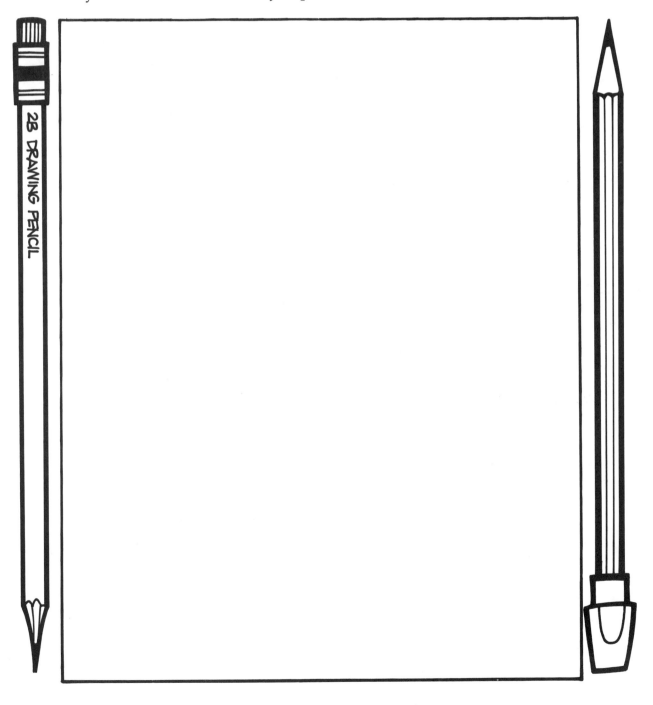

*The Box Book*
© The Learning Works, Inc.

# Favorite Character Collage

Cut out the sketch you have made of your favorite character. Draw around this shape on skin-tone construction paper. Add hair made from yarn or colored paper. Draw eyes, a mouth, and other features with crayons or markers, or create them out of paper. If your character wears glasses, you can draw them on or create them from yarn or pipe cleaners and glue them on.

When your collage is complete, mount it inside the lid of your cake box. Write the character's name below his or her face.

# Diorama Diagrams

favorite character collage

diorama in box

Glue one cake piece to the inside of each large lid flap.

Glue one cake piece to each of the four sides of the box.

fold

tab (apply glue here)

Each diorama piece should include a tab with which it may be attached inside the box.

47

# Fantasy Floats:
# To the Teacher

During the time between Thanksgiving and New Year's Day, many parades are televised and eagerly watched by millions. This is an especially appropriate time to make Fantasy Floats for your own classroom parade. Students will delight in recreating characters and settings from books they've read. They will also practice summarizing skills as they write story synopses for their floats. Take the completed floats "on the road" to share with other classrooms. Later, the floats can be put on display in your classroom or in the school library.

# Fantasy Floats

Everyone loves a parade! The theme for our classroom parade is "fantasy." Each float will star characters from a book that you have read.

## What You Need

Summary Sheet (page 52)
Float Diagrams (page 53)
Float Name Plaques (page 54)
shoe box
pencil
glue
tissue paper (5" x 12" strips and 1" squares, various colors)
construction paper (9" x 12" sheets, various colors)
oaktag (small pieces)
markers
scissors

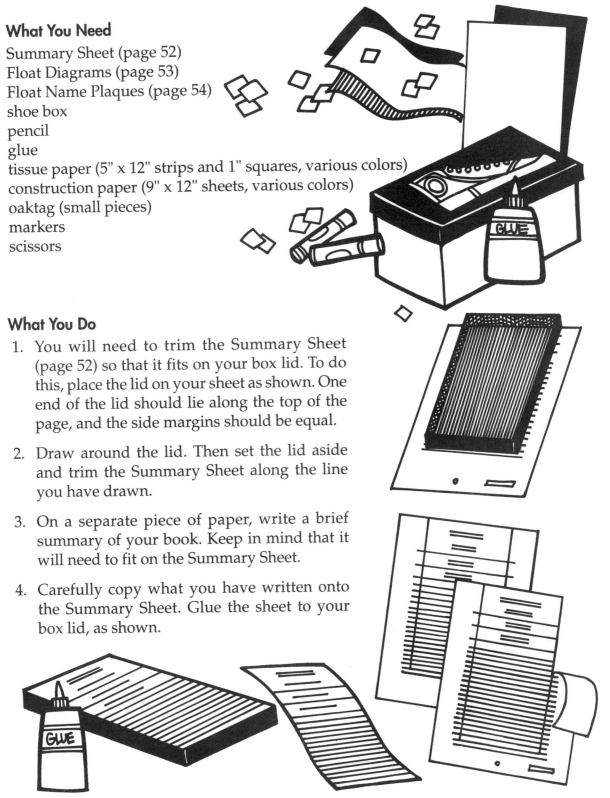

## What You Do

1. You will need to trim the Summary Sheet (page 52) so that it fits on your box lid. To do this, place the lid on your sheet as shown. One end of the lid should lie along the top of the page, and the side margins should be equal.

2. Draw around the lid. Then set the lid aside and trim the Summary Sheet along the line you have drawn.

3. On a separate piece of paper, write a brief summary of your book. Keep in mind that it will need to fit on the Summary Sheet.

4. Carefully copy what you have written onto the Summary Sheet. Glue the sheet to your box lid, as shown.

# Fantasy Floats
## continued

5. Fold your 5" x 12" tissue paper strips lengthwise, as shown. Cut each one along the open side to create fringe. Be careful not to cut all the way through.

6. Turn your box upside down. Glue your fringed strips around three sides of the box, as shown. Start at the bottom and add overlapping strips as you go up. Usually two or three rows are needed.

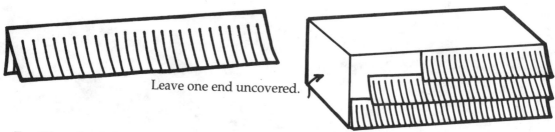

Leave one end uncovered.

7. Glue the lid to your shoe box, as shown.

8. Choose a favorite scene from your book. Select a piece of construction paper in a color that goes well with your scene (for example, green for grass or blue for water). Measure the bottom of the shoe box. Cut the construction paper to the exact size you measured. Glue the paper to the bottom of the shoe box.

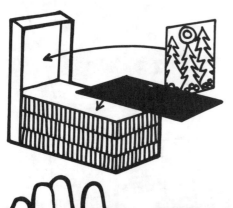

9. Cut out a piece of white paper to fit inside the lid of your shoe box. Draw and color a background for your scene on the paper and glue it in the box lid.

10. Cover the edge of the lid with tissue paper flowers. To make a flower, insert the eraser end of a pencil into a 1" x 1" tissue paper square and twist. Remove the pencil. Glue the flowers side by side, as shown.

# Fantasy Floats
## continued

11. Using oaktag, create a diorama of the scene that will stand up on the surface of the shoe box. (See the Float Diagrams on page 53.) Be sure to design each piece with a tab at the base so it can be glued securely to the float. Your pieces will look more complete if you design and color both the front and back of each item. Cut out your pieces and glue them to the bottom of the shoe box, as shown.

✱ For easier construction and stronger figures, do not cut out spaces such as these.

THE MOUNTAIN'S MELODY
BY ERICA ELROD

GLUE

12. Fill out both Float Name Plaques on page 54. Cut out and glue one on either side of your float.

13. You are now ready to enter your float in the classroom parade.

# Summary Sheet

Title of book

_____

Author

_____

Student's name

_____


_____

_____

_____

_____

_____

_____

_____

_____

_____

_____

_____

_____

_____

_____

_____

# Float Diagrams

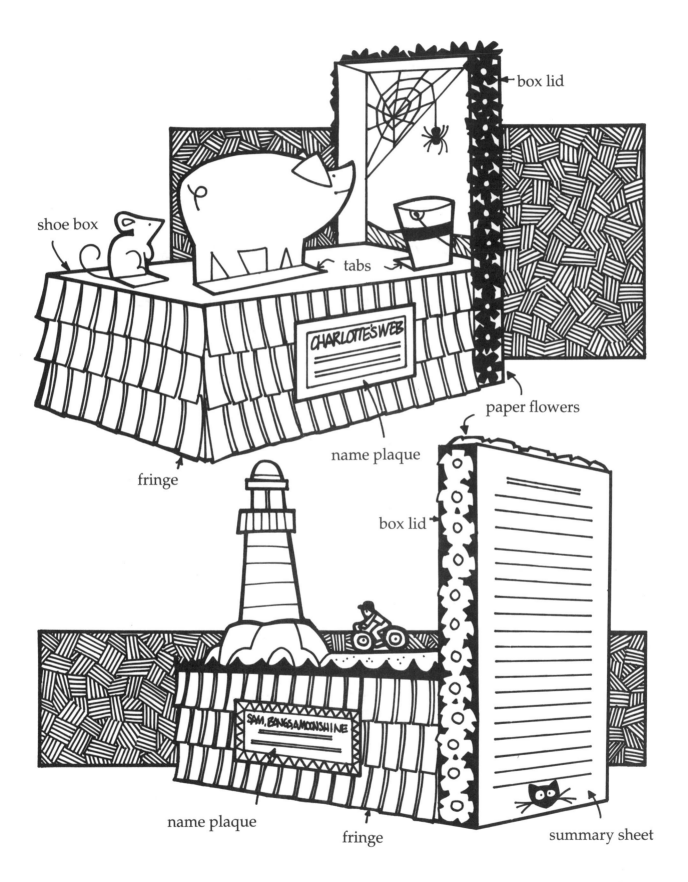

box lid

shoe box

tabs

CHARLOTTE'S WEB

paper flowers

name plaque

fringe

box lid

SAM, BANGS&MOONSHINE

name plaque

fringe

summary sheet

# Float Name Plaques

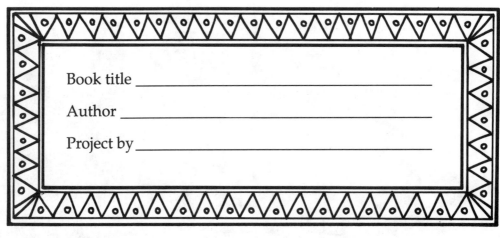

Book title _____

Author _____

Project by _____

Book title _____

Author _____

Project by _____

Winnie the Pooh
A.A. Milne
Courtney Ward

# Book Box Buddy:
# To the Teacher

Your students will love studying a favorite book character in depth for their Book Box Buddy. In the search for quotes about their chosen character, they will practice the skill of scanning for information. This is a great opportunity to teach the use of the ellipsis to indicate omission in direct quotations. The Book Box Buddies make a charming display for your classroom or school library.

The descriptions from the professional authors will serve as models as your students write their own character descriptions. Watch the fun as students exchange descriptions and draw each other's characters.

55

# Book Box Buddy

An author paints word pictures so vividly that you can see a book's characters in your mind. In this activity, you will search a book you have read for descriptive passages to help you create a "Book Box Buddy."

## What You Need

shoe box lid
pencil
Quote Book (page 57)
nontoxic paint
paintbrush
scissors
glue

two pieces of oaktag (8½" x 11")
Book Box Buddy Pattern (page 58)
Design a Character (page 59)
Paint a Word Picture (page 60)
markers
tape

## What You Do

1. Select a book to read. When you have finished reading, pick one character to be your Book Box Buddy.

2. Paint a shoe box lid.

3. Skim your book for passages that describe the personality and appearance of the character you have chosen. Use the Quote Book on page 57 to list these descriptive quotes and the page numbers on which they appear. Remember to use quotation marks.

4. Cut out and glue the Quote Book page to one of the pieces of oaktag. Fold the oaktag on the center line so it looks like a book. Secure it to the shoe box lid with tape, as shown.

5. Use the pattern on page 58 to make your Book Box Buddy. Cut out the pattern and draw around it in pencil on the other piece of oaktag.

6. Draw a face, hair, and clothing based on descriptions of this character in your book. Color your figure with markers and cut it out.

7. Bend your Book Box Buddy so it sits up, as shown. Glue it to the shoe box lid.

## Design a Character

- Now it's your turn to be the author. Design a character on page 59. Be creative. Your character may be realistic or a fantasy creature.

- Describe your character on page 60. You must "paint your word picture" so vividly that the reader will be able to see your character in his or her mind.

- Exchange descriptions with a classmate and draw each other's characters based on the word pictures.

# BOOK

Book Box Buddy:

Project by:

# QUOTE

Book title:

Author of book:

# Book Box Buddy Pattern

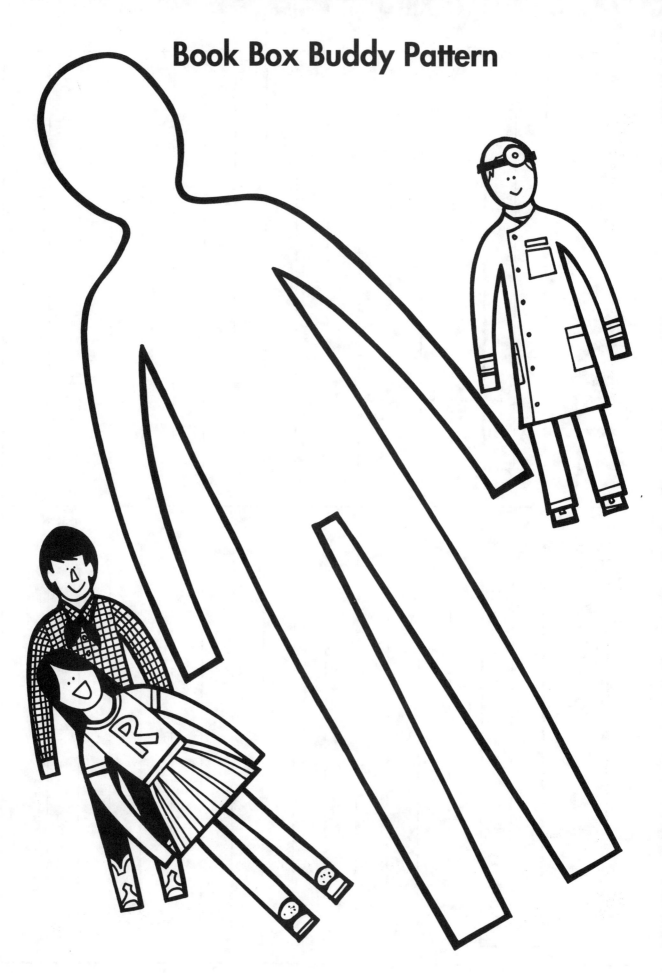

# Design a Character

Artist _____

*The Box Book*
© The Learning Works, Inc.

# Paint a Word Picture

On the lines below, write a paragraph describing your character.

_____

_____

_____

_____

_____

_____

_____

_____

_____

_____

_____

_____

_____

_____

_____

_____

_____

_____

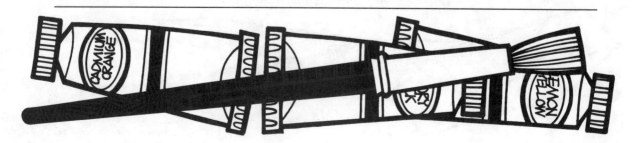

# Detective's Briefcase:
# To the Teacher

Select a class novel in the mystery genre, or allow students to choose their own novels. Show your students a completed sample of the Detective's Briefcase before beginning this project. You'll see the excitement build as your junior detectives begin to work on their briefcases on the first day of this project. The briefcases will serve as handy storage places for all of the activities. Demonstrate for your students how to pick out information in a novel that would be important to a detective. Teach the class how to take notes on the suspect(s), victim(s), evidence, and crime scene. Set up minimum standards on the amount of journal pages that each student should write. The children will need at least one stamp pad to make fingerprints on the cover of the detective's journal. Show students how to make fingerprints by rolling the finger from left to right so the prints don't smudge.

**Note:** This is a good time to teach or review writing in the first person. All of the work done in the journal should be from the point of view of the detective.

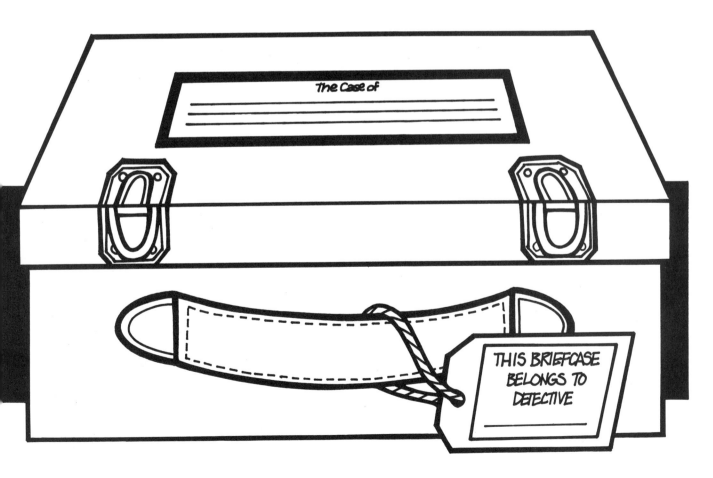

The Case of

THIS BRIEFCASE BELONGS TO DETECTIVE

*The Box Book*
© The Learning Works, Inc.

# Detective's Briefcase

Here's your chance to be a detective. In this activity you'll create everything a detective needs to solve a crime.

## What You Need

shoe box
brown nontoxic paint
paintbrush
crayons/markers (including gold and silver)
pencil
scissors
glue
yarn (6")
photo of yourself (approximately 3 x 2¹/₂")
Confidential Case Plaque and Diagram (page 64)
Handle, Latches, and Identification Tag (page 65)
Detective's I.D. Wallet (page 66)
Suspect(s), Victim(s), Evidence, and Crime Scene Journal (pages 67–70)
Detective's Journal Cover (page 71)
Sample Pages (72–73)
scratch paper
stamp pad
stapler
hole punch

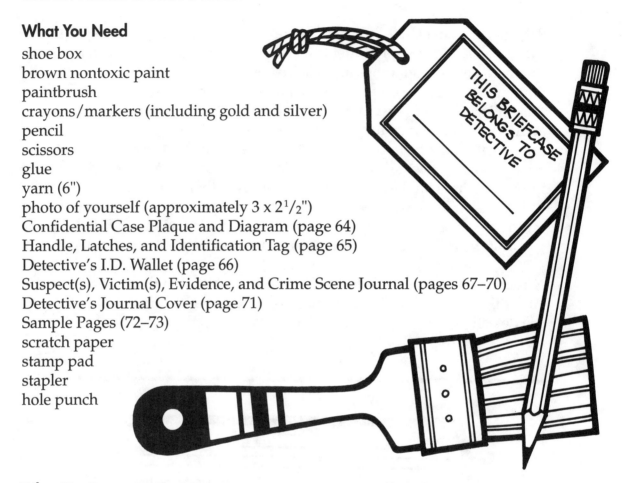

## What You Do

1. Paint the shoe box and set it aside until the paint is dry.

2. Fill out the information on the Confidential Case Plaque on page 64. Color it with markers, cut it out, and glue it to the top of the shoe box.

3. Put your name on the Identification Tag on page 65. Color the tag, the handle, and latches. Cut out the items, and glue them to the shoe box. Make sure the handle stands out, as shown. Punch out the hole in the Identification Tag, put the yarn through it, and attach it to the handle.

4. Color the background of the Detective's I.D. Wallet brown and the badge gold or silver. Glue a photo of yourself to the wallet, and write your name on the line provided. Cut the wallet out, fold it, and place it in your briefcase.

5. As you read your novel, jot down information that would be important to a detective trying to solve a case. Use scratch paper to write notes about the victim(s), suspect(s), evidence, and crime scene.

# Detective's Briefcase
## continued

After you have finished reading the novel and writing your notes, you will use the information you collected to complete the Detective's Journal (pages 67–70). Follow the directions provided below in steps 6–10. (Use scratch paper, if needed, to edit your notes and correct any mistakes.) Remember to write in first person, using "I" as if you were the detective. Look at the Sample Pages (pages 72–73) to see how your finished journal pages should look.

6. Use the **Suspect(s) and Victim(s) Journal Pages** to describe the characters in your novel. Include notes about their appearance and personality traits. In the space provided on the Suspect(s) Journal Page, draw a "mug shot" of the suspect(s). On the Victim(s) Journal Page, draw a picture of the victim(s). Use the author's descriptions in the book to make your pictures as accurate as possible. (Do your drawings in black and white so they will look more like real police sketches.)

7. Use the **Crime Scene Journal Page** to describe the setting in important action scenes. Use the author's descriptions to help you draw an accurate black-and-white "photo" of the crime scene.

8. Use the **Evidence Journal Page** to describe any evidence that the detective has found. At home, make 3-D models to include in the briefcase. Be inventive! You can make a "diamond" ring from aluminum foil or make a document look old by staining it with tea.

9. After you have completed the journal pages, color the Detective's Journal Cover (page 71) with crayons or markers. Cut out the cover and the journal pages. Staple the journal pages to the cover.

10. Your teacher will provide a stamp pad. Use the pad to make fingerprints in the magnifying glass on the Detective's Journal Cover.

11. Put the finished journal in the briefcase.

12. Your detective's briefcase is now complete. It should include your Detective's I.D. Wallet, your Detective's Journal, and the 3-D models of the evidence.

*The Box Book*
© The Learning Works, Inc.

# Confidential Case Plaque and Diagram

### The Case of

Book title _____

Author _____

Detective _____

## Detective's Briefcase Diagram

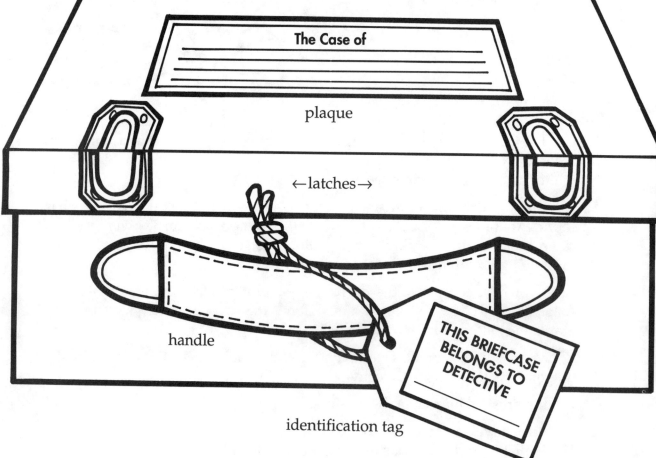

### The Case of

plaque

←latches→

handle

THIS BRIEFCASE BELONGS TO DETECTIVE _____

identification tag

# Handle, Latches, and Identification Tag

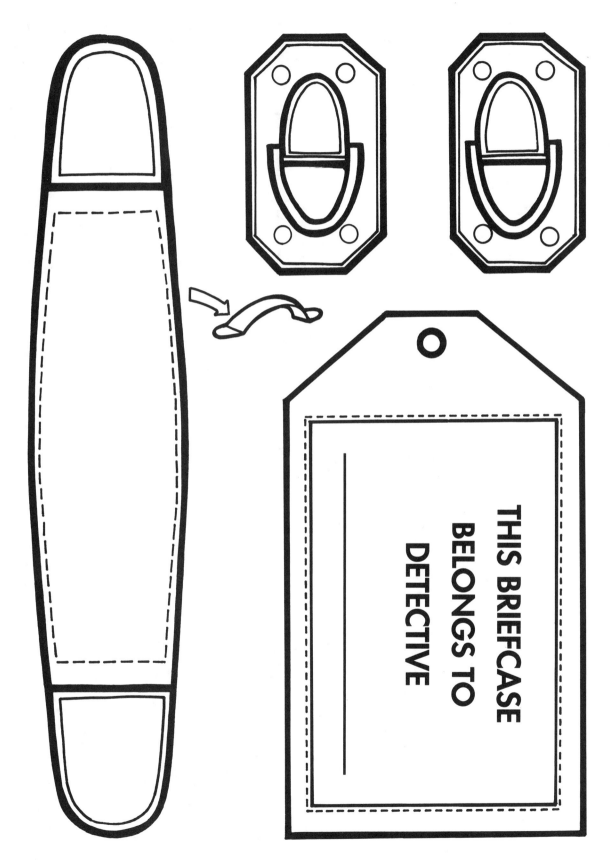

THIS BRIEFCASE
BELONGS TO
DETECTIVE

*The Box Book*
© The Learning Works, Inc.

# Detective's I.D. Wallet

cut along solid line

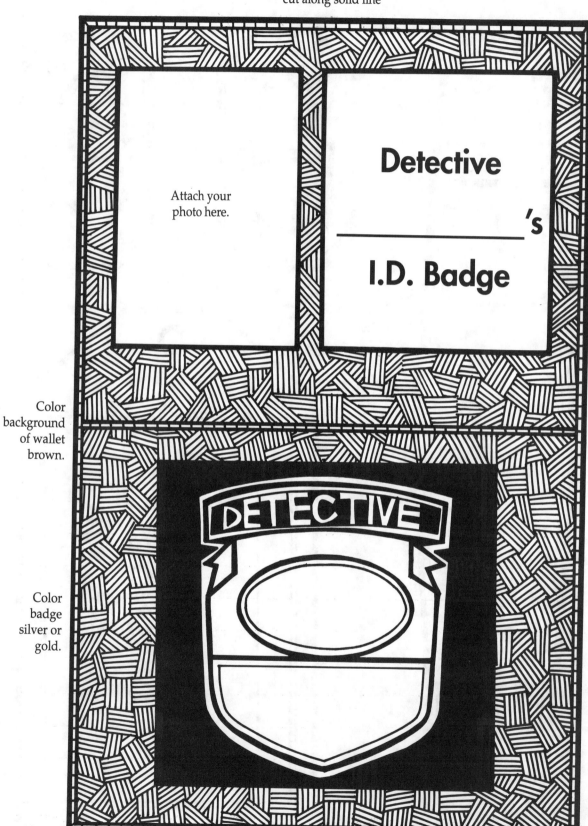

Attach your
photo here.

## Detective

_____'s

## I.D. Badge

Color
background
of wallet
brown.

fold

Color
badge
silver or
gold.

DETECTIVE

# Suspect(s) Journal Page

### Notes on Suspect(s)

_____

_____

_____

_____

_____

_____

_____

_____

_____

_____

_____

_The Box Book_
© The Learning Works, Inc.

# Victim(s) Journal Page

### Notes on Victim(s)

_____

_____

_____

_____

_____

_____

_____

_____

_____

_____

_____

# Evidence Journal Page

## Notes on Evidence

_____

_____

_____

_____

_____

_____

_____

_____

_____

_____

_____

_____

_____

_____

_____

_____

_____

_____

# Crime Scene Journal Page

**Notes on the Crime Scene**

_____

_____

_____

_____

_____

_____

_____

_____

_____

_____

_____

**CONFIDENTIAL JOURNAL**

**PERSONAL PROPERTY
OF DETECTIVE**

*The Box Book*
© The Learning Works, Inc.

# Sample Page

## Crime Scene Journal Page

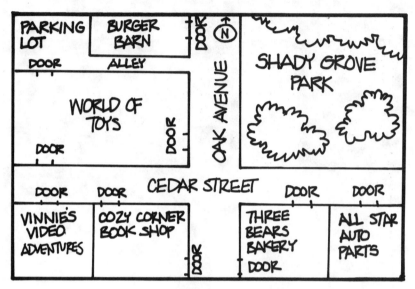

**Notes on the Crime Scene**

This is part of Eagle Creek. Many things have been stolen from World of Toys. Vinnie says that twenty-two of his videos are missing. There are lots of hiding places in the bushes and trees at the park. Billy Brown is often seen near this intersection. He doesn't live near here, but the school he goes to is just three blocks north. The police department is three miles away.

# Sample Page

## Suspect(s) Journal Page

### Notes on Suspect(s)

Billy Brown, a fifth-grader, is the bully of Eagle Creek Elementary School. All of the other students are afraid of him. He has brown eyes and light brown hair, and is tall for his age. Billy rides a red mountain bike and is usually wearing a black baseball cap. Sometimes he goes by the nickname "Big Bill." Look for him at the Burger Barn or Vinnie's Video Adventures.

*The Box Book*
© The Learning Works, Inc.

# Mathematical Doctor:
# To the Teacher

This activity is a great way to teach and reinforce vocabulary for the four basic operations. Ask the students to challenge themselves when writing sample problems.

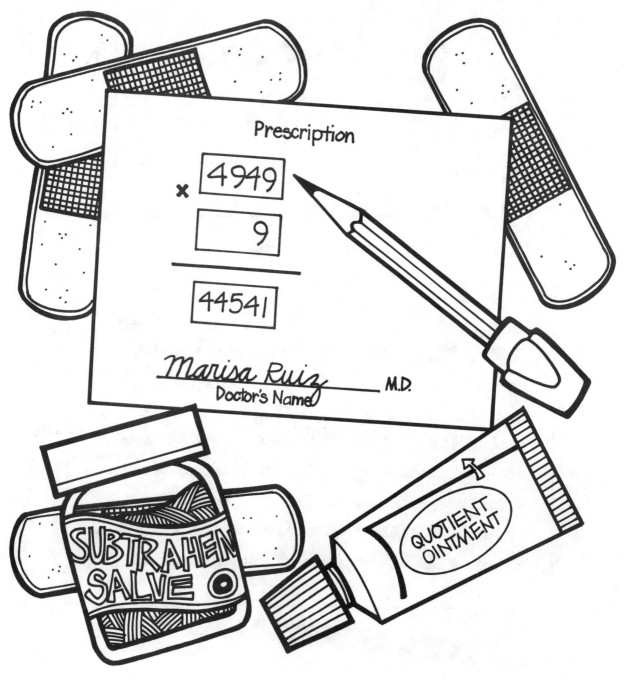

# Mathematical Doctor

Enjoy being a mathematical doctor as you practice using the vocabulary for the four basic operations and write prescriptions for a game with your friends.

**What You Need**

Medical Kit (page 77)
Math Vocabulary Page (page 78)
pencil
markers
black or brown construction paper
   (12" x 18" and 9" x 12")
cardboard bandage box
glue
scissors
ruler
Handles and Buckle (page 79)
Label and Medical Symbol (page 80)
Prescription Flashcards (page 81; three copies per student)

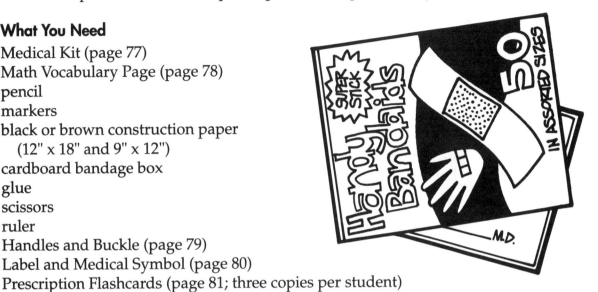

**What You Do**

1. Color the contents of the Medical Kit on page 77.

2. Make up four math problems which show addition, subtraction, multiplication, and division. Carefully copy these problems into the boxes on the Math Vocabulary Page (page 78). Check your work to make sure your answers are correct.

3. Make a set of parallel lines the width of the bandage box in the middle of the construction paper. Fold the construction paper along these lines to make a spine for the doctor's bag, as shown.

4. Cut along the dotted lines on pages 77 and 78 to trim away the excess paper. Glue the remaining shapes to your construction paper, as shown.

5. Draw a line 1/2" beyond the edges of the glued-on shapes, as shown. Then cut along this line.

# Mathematical Doctor
## continued

6. Glue the bandage box to the Medical Kit page.

7. Color the handles and buckle on page 79. Glue them to construction paper, then cut them out. Attach the handles and buckle to the doctor's bag.

8. Write your name on the label on page 80. Color the medical symbol. Cut these pieces out and glue them to the bag, as shown.

### Preparing to Play and Game Rules

• Cut out the prescription flashcards (page 81). Use your skills as a mathematical doctor to prescribe practice problems for your classmates. On each flashcard, write a problem showing one of the four basic operations. You have 12 flashcards, so make three examples of each operation. On each card, circle a different part of the operation (sum, factor, quotient, etc.).

• Sign your name on the line provided on each Prescription Flashcard. Put the cards into the bandage box until you are ready to play the game.

**Game Rules**

• Two students take turns being doctor and patient. The doctor holds up one of his or her flashcards, and the patient tries to identify the circled part.

• If the patient is right, the patient gets the card. If the patient is incorrect, the doctor keeps the card. (Check the answers by using the Math Vocabulary Page).

• The game ends when all of the flashcards have been shown. The player with the most cards is the winner!

# Medical Kit

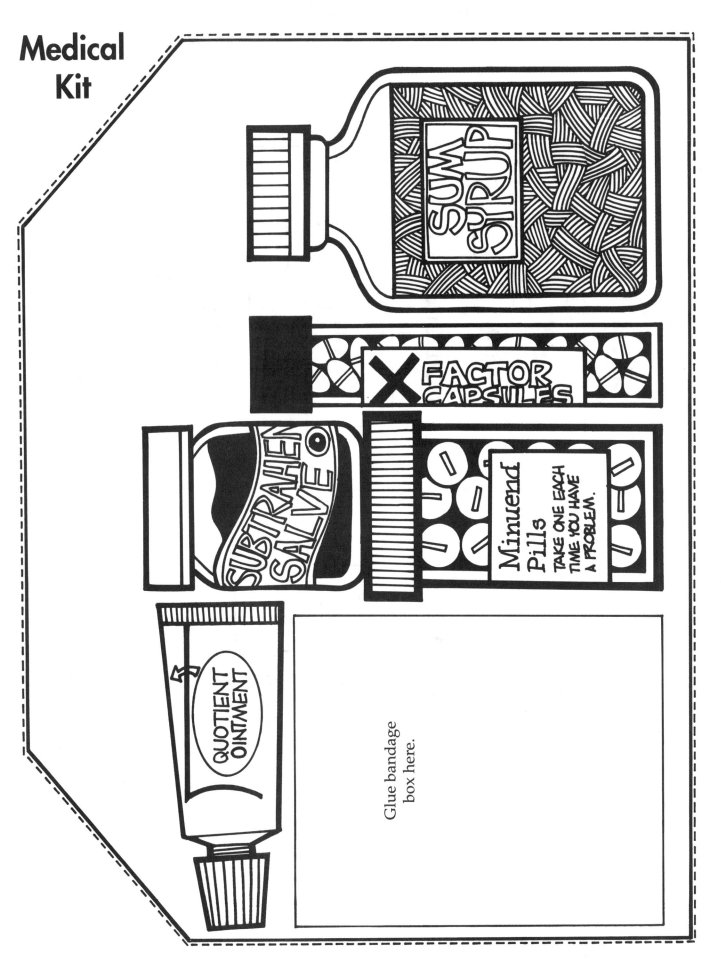

SUMP SYRUP

X FACTOR CAPSULES

SUBTRAHEND SALVE

Minuend Pills
TAKE ONE EACH TIME YOU HAVE A PROBLEM.

QUOTIENT OINTMENT

Glue bandage box here.

# Math Vocabulary Page

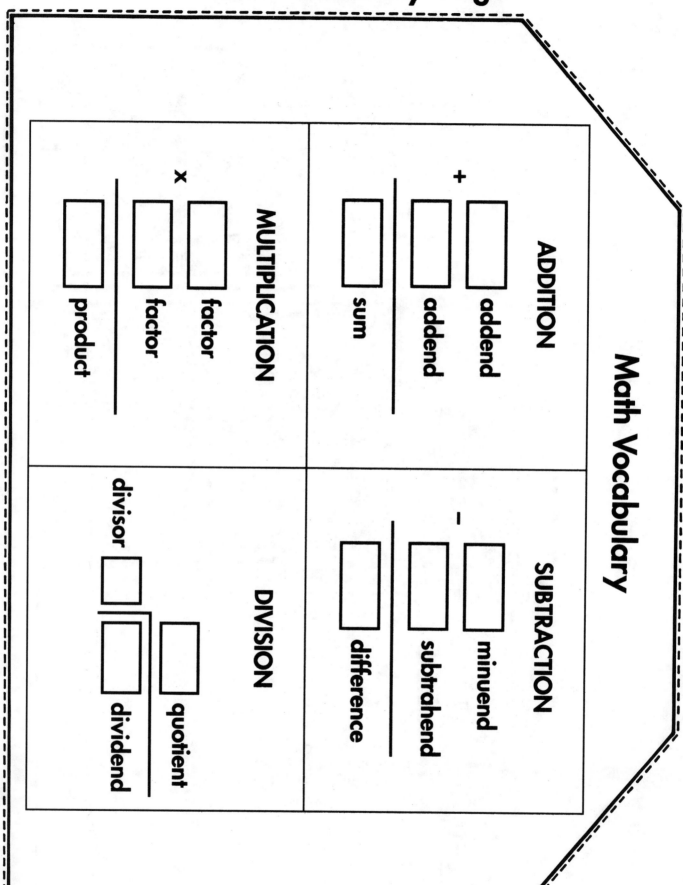

**Math Vocabulary**

**ADDITION**

+

addend
addend
sum

**MULTIPLICATION**

×

factor
factor
product

**SUBTRACTION**

−

minuend
subtrahend
difference

**DIVISION**

divisor
quotient
dividend

# Handles and Buckle

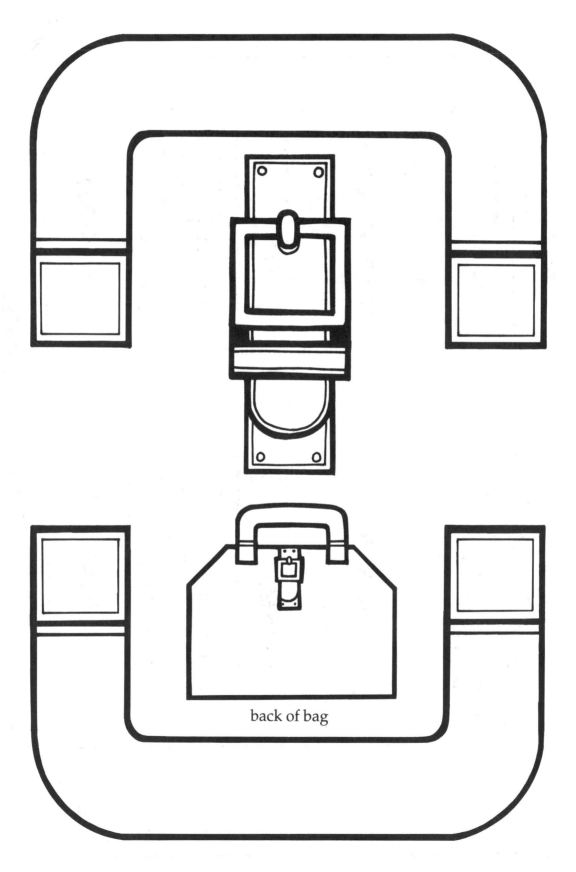

back of bag

*The Box Book*
© The Learning Works, Inc.

# Label and Medical Symbol

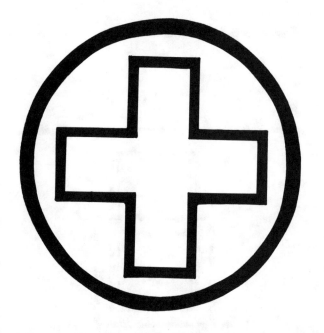

_____ **M.D.**

## MATHEMATICAL DOCTOR

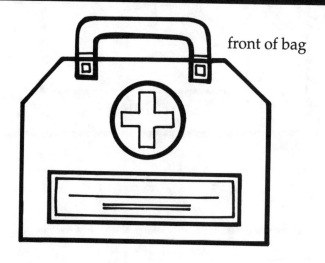

front of bag

# Prescription Flashcards

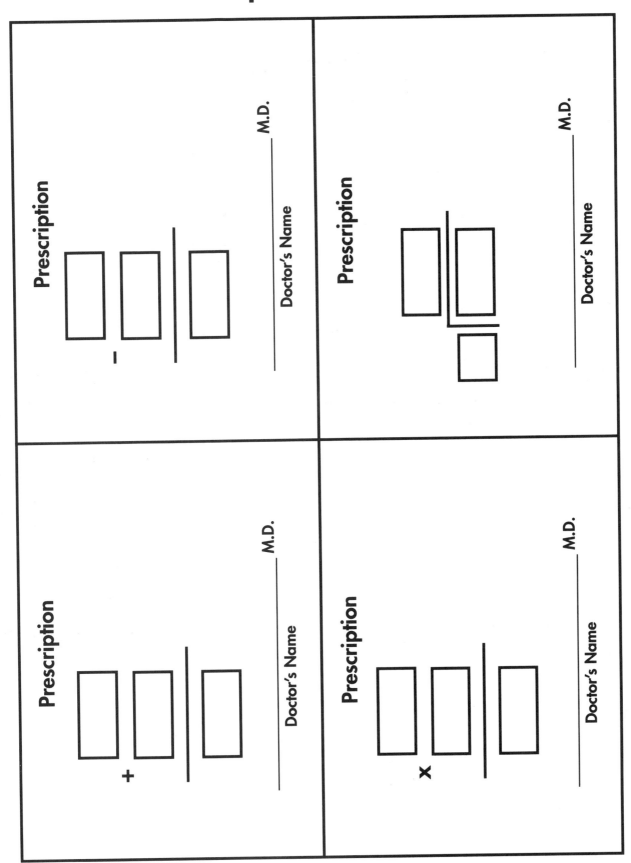

# Math Rap:
# To the Teacher

In this activity, students will practice brainstorming and write lyrics that incorporate math concepts. This is a great time to teach or review meter, couplets, and rhyming patterns. After they have written their Map Raps, students can perform them for their classmates. Students who are a little shy may feel more comfortable if they are allowed to perform with partners or in a group. Kids enjoy dressing up for this activity. As a culmination of this activity, hold a "concert day" and let all of your budding rap artists perform their Math Raps.

# Math Rap

It's time to pump up the volume! Here's your chance to become a rap artist, write the next chart-topping hit and create your own CD!

## What You Need

pencil
Math Rap Example (page 84)
Math Rap Lyric Sheet (page 85)
CD Cover (page 86)
markers
scissors
plastic CD box
CD Brainstorm (pages 87–88)

## What You Do

1. Brainstorm a list of math words on a piece of scratch paper. If you need help, sneak a peek at the glossary of your math book.

2. You may write your rap as a solo, or you may work with a partner. In your rap, try to incorporate as many math words as you can. Look at the Math Rap Example on page 84. On a separate piece of paper, write a rough draft of your Math Rap. Revise and edit your work.

3. Write the final copy of your rap on the Math Rap Lyric Sheet on page 85.

4. Design a cover for your CD on page 86. Color your cover and cut it out. Slip it into the front of the plastic CD box.

5. Now imagine you're a famous rap artist. Using the CD outlines on pages 87–88, practice brainstorming by listing all the places you'll perform, the artists who will play with you, the songs you'll write, and the things you'll buy or the people you'll help with the money you earn.

6. Cut out the CDs and put them inside the CD box.

7. Practice your rap. Perform it for your classmates. And have a pen handy for signing autographs!

*The Box Book*
© The Learning Works, Inc.

# Math Rap Example

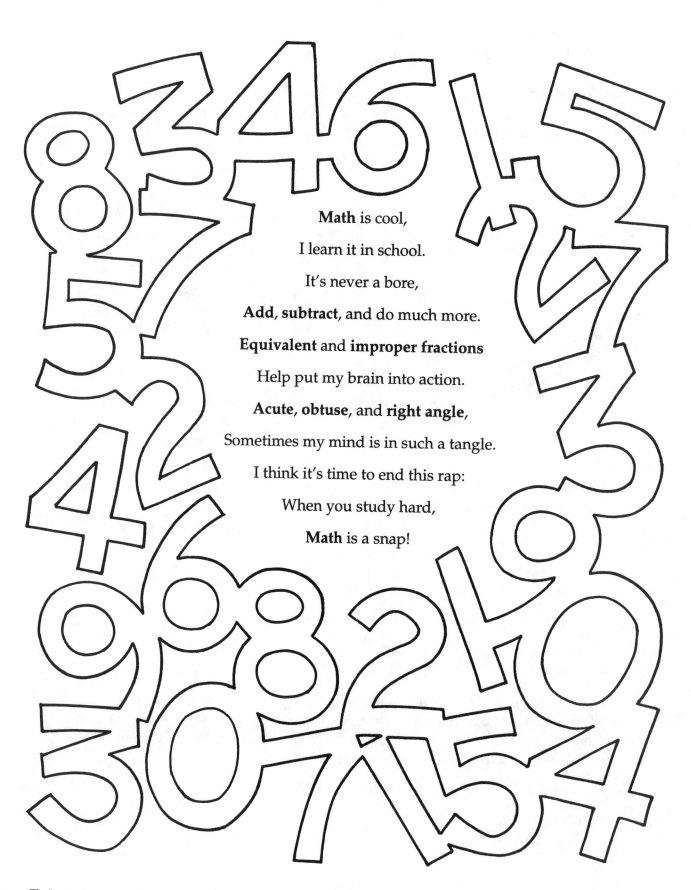

Math is cool,

I learn it in school.

It's never a bore,

Add, subtract, and do much more.

Equivalent and improper fractions

Help put my brain into action.

Acute, obtuse, and right angle,

Sometimes my mind is in such a tangle.

I think it's time to end this rap:

When you study hard,

Math is a snap!

# Math Rap Lyric Sheet

Artist _____

_____
_____
_____
_____
_____
_____
_____
_____
_____
_____
_____
_____
_____
_____
_____
_____
_____
_____
_____
_____
_____

# CD Cover

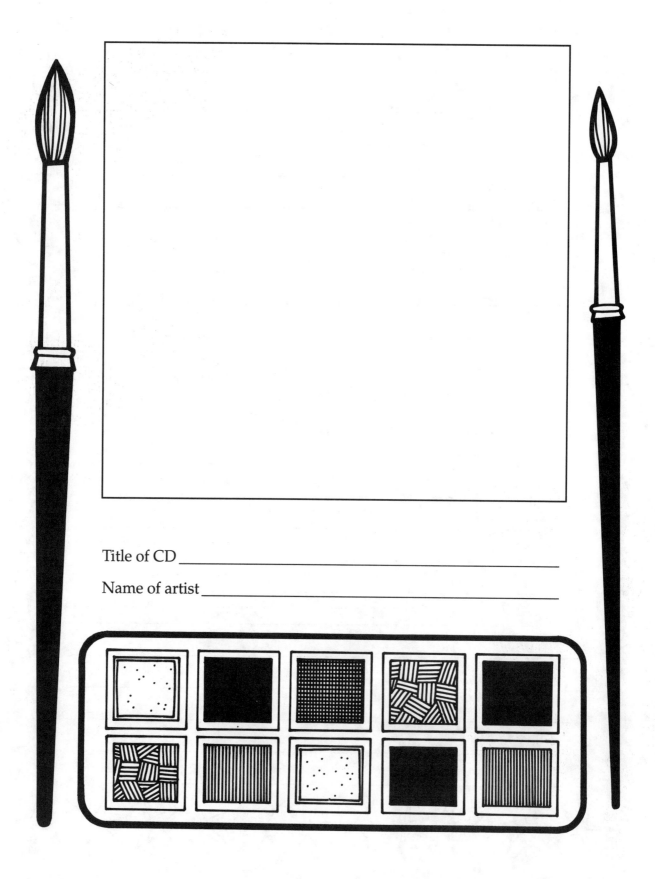

Title of CD _____

Name of artist _____

# CD Brainstorm

**Places**

1. _____
2. _____
3. _____
4. _____
5. _____
6. _____
7. _____
8. _____
9. _____

_____

**Name**

**Artists**

1. _____
2. _____
3. _____
4. _____
5. _____
6. _____
7. _____
8. _____
9. _____

_____

**Name**

# CD Brainstorm

## Songs

1. _____
2. _____
3. _____
4. _____
5. _____
6. _____
7. _____
8. _____
9. _____
_____

**Name**

## Spending or Helping Spree

1. _____
2. _____
3. _____
4. _____
5. _____
6. _____
7. _____
8. _____
9. _____
_____

**Name**

# Author Box:
# To the Teacher

Researching favorite authors can help children see them as "real people" with full and interesting lives. Books, magazines, and the Internet are good sources for biographical information. And most children's librarians are familiar with the work and lives of classic and current authors.

This project will give students a chance to develop or practice research skills and to learn more about authors whose work they admire. Discovering common interests and experiences helps children feel a kinship with their literary heroes. Imagine finding out that your favorite author grew up in your state, likes soccer, and once had a little brother as exasperating as your own!

When completed, these author boxes make an attractive, interactive classroom or library display that invites students to learn about a variety of authors.

Patterns for an invitation and a poster for your display are included in this unit.

My favorite quote from this author is "hundreds of cats, thousands of cats, millions and billions and trillions of cats."

This author's first book

GUESS WHO EACH AUTHOR IS. THEN PULL OUT THE TAG TO DISCOVER HIS OR HER NAME.

This author is also an artist. He works at home in a room full of books, animals, and art supplies. Lots of kids hang out at his house, and he doesn't mind. He lives in California and has a pool. I'd like to live next door!

Some of this author's books are Huge Harold, The Whingdingdilly, Kermit the Hermit, The Gnats of Knotty Pine, Capyboppy, Big Bad Bruce, & Eli. I have read all of those books!

# Author Box

Do you have some favorite authors? You may have read and reread their books, but know little about the authors themselves. When were they born? Where did they grow up? What were their families like? If they are still alive, what are their interests? Do they go camping, have pets, or play chess?

Choose an author and do some research to find out about him or her. Then make an Author Box to record and share what you have learned.

## What You Need

About the Author (pages 91–92)
empty tissue box, $4^{1}/_{4}$" x $4^{1}/_{4}$" x $5^{1}/_{4}$"
Author Box Side Pattern
 (page 93; four copies per student)
Author Box Top and Tag Patterns (page 94)
scissors
glue
pen and/or pencil
markers and/or crayons
2" x 7" strip of construction paper
10" piece of yarn
hole punch

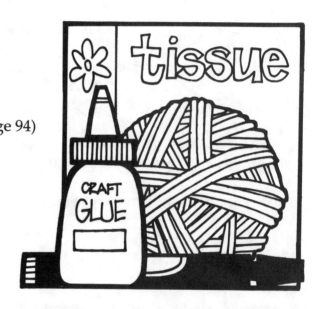

## What You Do

1. Choose a favorite author to learn about. Do research on him or her using books, the Internet, or other reference sources. Take notes on your About the Author pages.

2. Color and complete the four side patterns, following the directions on page 93. Glue the patterns to the sides of your box.

3. If the hole in your tissue box is covered with plastic, carefully remove the plastic.

4. Prepare the box top pattern, following the directions on page 94. Glue the pattern to your box.

5. Write your author's name on the tag pattern. Color the tag and cut it out. Glue it to your construction paper strip. Punch a hole and add the yarn.

6. Put the tag inside your Author Box. Share your box with others. See if they can identify the author without looking at the tag.

Name _____

# About the Author

Use these pages (91–92) for note-taking as you do research on your author. (Don't worry if you can't find all of this information.) Write the most interesting facts that you find on the side panels of your Author Box.

Author's name _____

Does he or she have a nickname or pen name?

_____

Where and when was this person born?

_____

Tell about your author's childhood interests and experiences.

Is this author still alive?

☐ Yes ☐ No

_____

_____

_____

_____

_____

_____

_____

_____

What work has this person done other than writing?

_____

_____

_____

_____

_____

_____

_____

Name _____

# About the Author
## continued

Is this author married? Does he or she have children?

_____

_____

_____

What book or books has this person written? Has he or she authored plays, poems, or magazine articles?

_____

_____

_____

_____

_____

 Has this author received any special awards?

_____

_____

_____

What cities, states, and/or countries has this person lived in?

_____

_____

What are some of your author's interests and activities?

_____

_____

_____

_____

Copy a quote by your author below.

_____

_____

_____

_____

_____

_____

# Author Box Side Pattern

You will need four copies of this page (one for each side of your Author Box).

In each of the eight rectangles, write an interesting fact that you learned about your author. (Refer to your notes on pages 91–92.)

Color the borders around the rectangles. You may wish to add designs like the ones below.

Cut out your patterns, and glue one to each side of your Author Box.

**To the teacher:** Before reproducing this page, you may wish to draw lines—spaced appropriately for your students to write on—in the two rectangles.

*The Box Book*
© The Learning Works, Inc.

# Author Box Top and Tag Patterns

Color your box top pattern and write your name on it.

Cut out the pattern.

To cut out the hole, first fold the pattern as shown.

Start cutting at the fold, then follow along the dotted line.

Glue the top to your box.

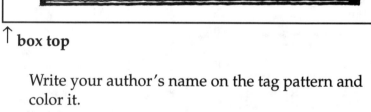

↑ **box top**

Write your author's name on the tag pattern and color it.

Cut out your tag pattern and glue it to the construction paper strip.

Punch a hole where indicated and attach the yarn as shown.

Put the tag in your Author Box.

↓ **tag**

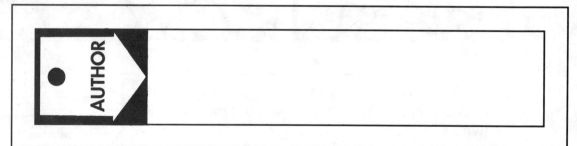

# Box Display Invitation

Date _____

Dear _____,

In class, we have been learning lots of interesting things about our favorite authors:

- when and where they were born
- their childhoods
- their interests and hobbies
- their jobs
- their families
- the places where they have lived

We have made a great display to share the things we have learned, and we invite you to come see it!

Sincerely,

_____

```
DATE, TIME, AND PLACE OF DISPLAY



```

*The Box Book*
© The Learning Works, Inc.

# Box Display Poster

**COME TO OUR**

**AUTHOR BOX**

**DISPLAY!**

- **Find out more about your favorite authors, and meet some new ones.**

- **Read the clues, and guess who's who!**

| PRESENTED BY |
| --- |
|  |

| WHEN AND WHERE |
| --- |
|  |

AUTHOR

Hugh

This author was a soldier in World War I, where he saw many animals getting hurt.

When this author wrote to his children back home, he told them funny stories about a doctor who helped animals.

# Shoe Box Time Line:
# To the Teacher

This social studies activity emphasizes the chronological order of historical events. Each student will select 10 important historical events and research them using a variety of sources. The student will then make a drawing of each event and put these illustrations in chronological order. The time line thus created is an exciting project for sharing with other classes—either as part of a standing display or "taken on tour" by the young historian who created it.

*The Box Book*
© The Learning Works, Inc.

# Shoe Box Time Line

Open up this shoe box and take a "walk through history" as historical events unfold in chronological order.

## What You Need

research sources (the Internet, encyclopedias, and other reference books)
Time Line Diagram (page 99)
Time Line Worksheet (page 100)
Time Line Form (page 101;
    10 copies per student)
Time Line Cover (page 102)
painted or covered shoe box
colored pencils or markers
scissors
tape
pencil

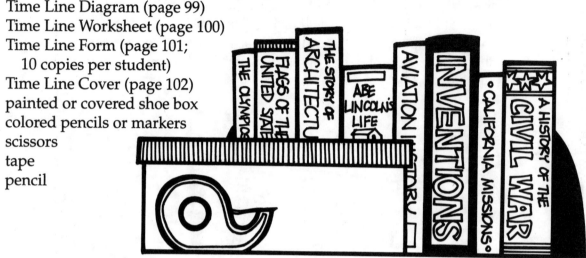

## What You Do

1.  Using research sources such as the Internet, encyclopedias, and other reference books, investigate a series of 10 important events in history.

2.  List the events in chronological order on the Time Line Worksheet on page 100.

3.  When you have completed your research and filled out the Worksheet, your teacher will give you 10 Time Line Forms—one for each event.

4.  On each form, draw a picture of one of the events you have chosen. Use colored pens or markers. Add the name and date(s) of the event.

5.  Cut out the forms and tape each sheet to the next in chronological order, as shown in the diagram on page 99.

6.  Fill in the Time Line Cover on page 102. Create a design for the cover which represents the events you have researched.

7.  Color the cover, cut it out, and tape it to the lid of your shoe box.

8.  Fold the Time Line Forms in and out like a fan along the dotted lines, as shown in the diagram on page 99.

9.  Attach the ends of your Time Line to the shoe box. Tape the last panel inside the box, and fasten the side of the first panel to the lid.

10. Share your walk through history with your classmates and others.

# Time Line Diagram

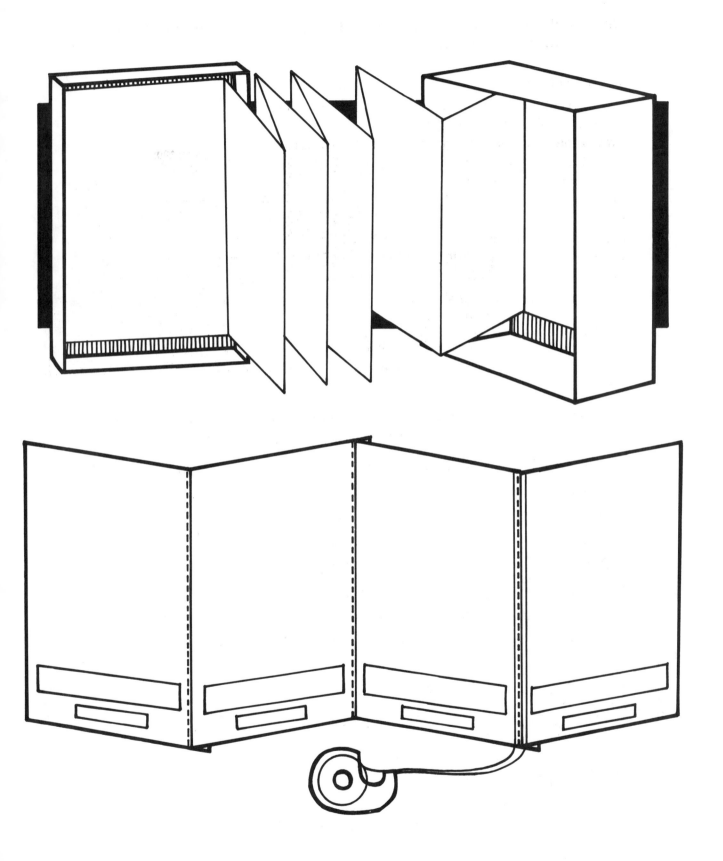

*The Box Book*
© The Learning Works, Inc.

# Time Line Worksheet

List events in chronological order.

Date(s)

1. _____  _____

2. _____  _____

3. _____  _____

4. _____  _____

5. _____  _____

6. _____  _____

7. _____  _____

8. _____  _____

9. _____  _____

10. _____  _____

# Time Line Form

Duplicate as needed.

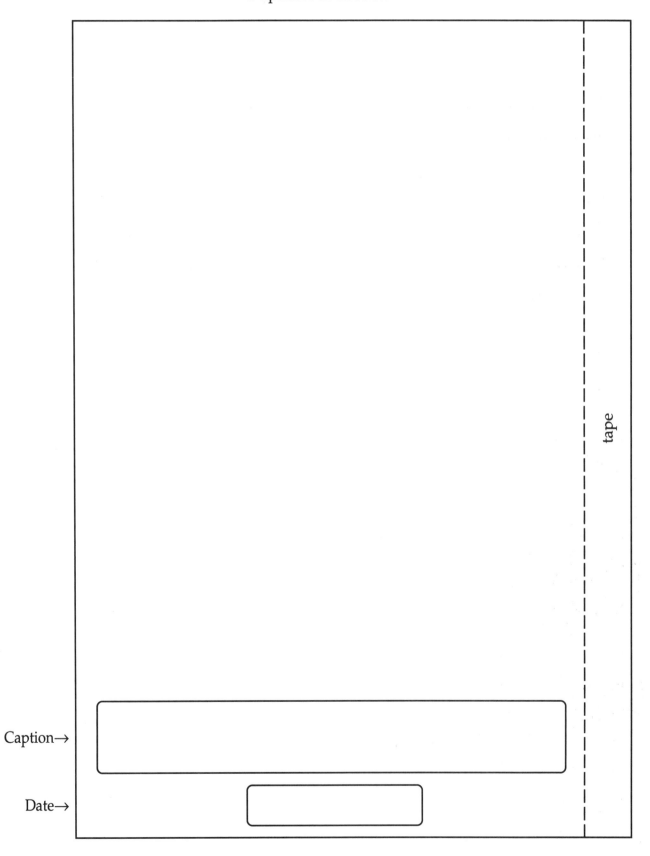

tape

Caption→

Date→

*The Box Book*
© The Learning Works, Inc.

# Time Line Form

Cut along dotted line.

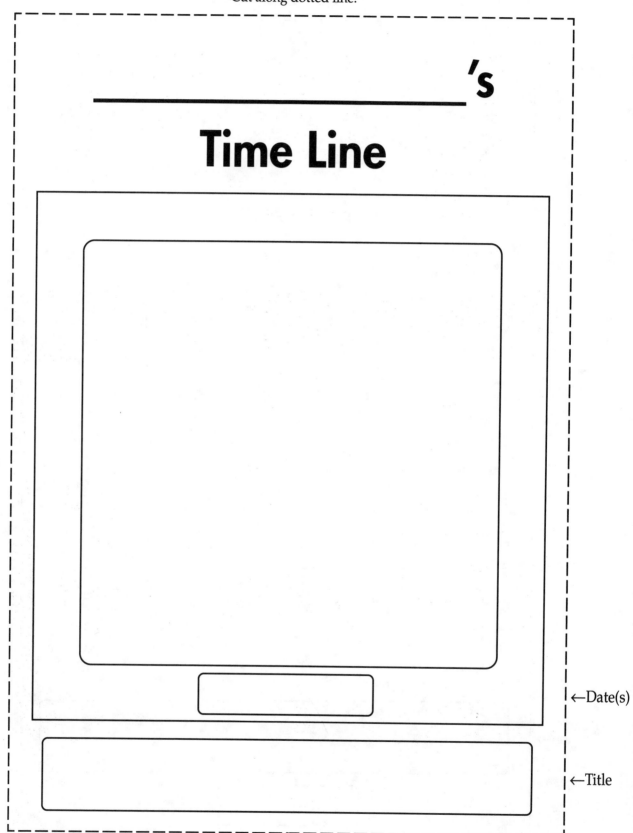

_____'s

## Time Line

←Date(s)

←Title

# Shoe Box Sea Chest:
# To the Teacher

In this science activity, students explore the mysteries of the ocean by combining scientific facts with creative thinking. Each student gathers 10 scientific facts about the ocean using resources such as books, encyclopedias, magazines, and the Internet, and enters this information in a Scientific Journal. Using these facts, the student creates a Captain's Log in which he or she describes a fictitious six-day underwater adventure. The Captain's Log and student-created "ocean specimens" are then locked away in a shoe box the student has decorated to look like an old sea chest.

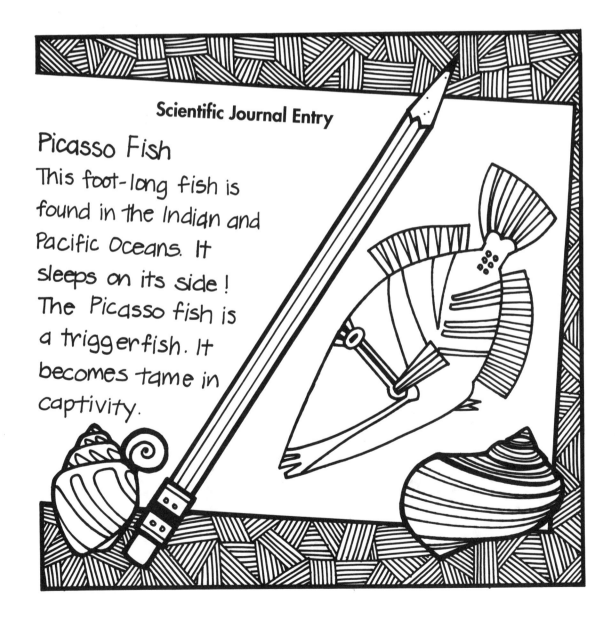

**Scientific Journal Entry**

Picasso Fish

This foot-long fish is found in the Indian and Pacific Oceans. It sleeps on its side! The Picasso fish is a triggerfish. It becomes tame in captivity.

# Shoe Box Sea Chest

Ahoy captains! Get ready to command a submarine on an exciting trip to investigate the ocean's depths. While traveling, you will have the opportunity to research some important facts and keep a log of your adventures. When you arrive back at port, you will lock your log in a sea chest for safekeeping.

## What You Need

research sources (books, magazines, and the Internet)
notebook paper
pencil
markers
scissors
Captain's Log Cover (page 106)
Scientific Journal Entry Forms (page 107)
stapler
Captain's Log Daily Entry Forms (page 108)
New Specimen Entry Form (page 109)
stapler
student-created "ocean specimens"
covered or painted shoe box
Marine Life Clip Art (page 110)
Handle and Hinge Patterns (page 111)
Lock and Label Patterns (page 112)
glue

## What You Do

1. Investigate scientific facts about the ocean and its inhabitants using a variety of research sources such as books, magazines, and the Internet.

2. On a sheet of notebook paper, record 10 scientific facts. Carefully edit your work.

3. Put your name on the Captain's Log Cover on page 106. Color and cut it out.

# Shoe Box Sea Chest
## continued

4. Your teacher will give you 10 Scientific Journal Entry forms. Using your edited notes, write one scientific fact on each form. Draw a picture to accompany each fact. Cut the forms apart.

5. Your teacher will give you six Captain's Log Daily Entry forms. Write six entries describing the exciting adventures you had as the captain of the submarine. Include the real facts from the Scientific Journal Entry forms in your descriptions. More than one scientific fact can be used in each Daily Entry.

6. Cut the Daily Entry forms apart. Fill out the New Specimen Entry form on page 109. Illustrate this form and cut it out.

7. Gather the Captain's Log Cover, Scientific Journal Entries, Captain's Log Daily Entries, and the New Specimen Entry, and staple them together to create a booklet. You have now completed your Captain's Log.

8. Draw pictures or create 3-D models of ocean specimens, such as shells, small fishes, and starfishes. Think about your adventure. Include items that you described in your Captain's Log Daily Entries. Use the Marine Life Clip Art on page 110.

9. Paint or cover a shoe box to look like an old sea chest.

10. Make handles and hinges for the chest using the pattern on page 111 and a lock using the pattern on page 112. Attach these items to the chest, as shown.

11. Fill out the sea chest label (page 112). Cut it out and glue it to the lid of the chest.

12. Place the Captain's Log and your "ocean specimens" in the sea chest. Share your sea chest with your classmates.

*The Box Book*
© The Learning Works, Inc.

# Captain's Log Cover

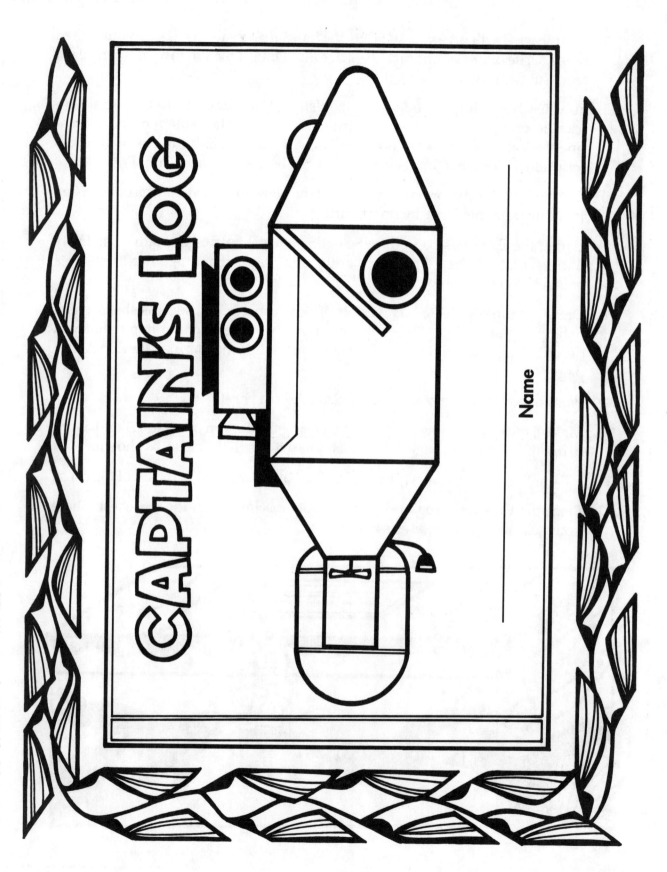

# Scientific Journal Entry Forms

## Scientific Journal Entry

_____

_____

_____

_____

_____

_____

_____

_____

_____

## Scientific Journal Entry

_____

_____

_____

_____

_____

_____

_____

_____

_____

_The Box Book_
© The Learning Works, Inc.

# Captain's Log Daily Entry Forms

## Captain's Log Daily Entry

**Day** [ ]

_____
_____
_____
_____
_____
_____
_____

_____
Captain

## Captain's Log Daily Entry

**Day** [ ]

_____
_____
_____
_____
_____
_____
_____

_____
Captain

# New Specimen Entry Form

Imagine that you and your crew discover a whole new species of underwater creature on your voyage. Sketch and describe the new specimen below.

### New Specimen Entry

Captain

Date of first sighting

# Marine Life Clip Art

# Handle and Hinge Patterns

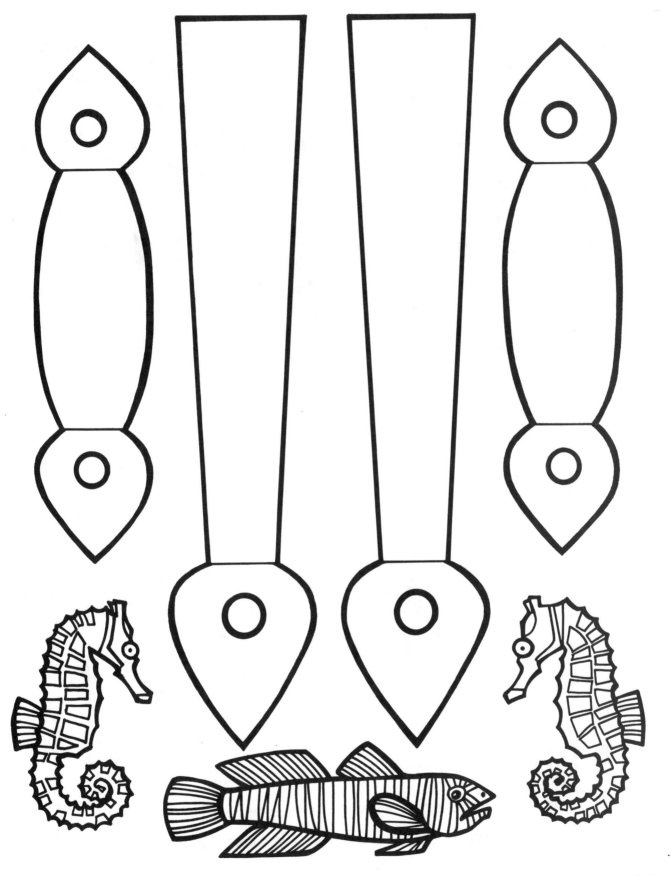

111

# Lock and Label Patterns

Glue on edge of lid.

Cut here.→

Glue on box.

PRIVATE
PROPERTY
OF CAPTAIN

# Mini-Menagerie:
# To the Teacher

Most children are fascinated by the insects, spiders, and other tiny animals found living in yards, parks, and vacant lots. In this project, students will research their favorite "critters" and then create displays showing these animals in their natural habitats.

Making a Mini-Menagerie combines research and writing skills with art, science, and fun! This project can easily be adapted for older and younger students.

*The Box Book*
© The Learning Works, Inc.

# Mini-Menagerie

A *menagerie* is a zoo—a collection of animals. Many zoo animals are large and exotic, but tiny, familiar critters can be just as interesting. Did you know that the daddy longlegs can taste and smell with its legs, or that the garden snail has 15,000 teeth on its tongue?

Choose a critter from pages 116–119, research it, and record your findings on the Critter Information sheet (page 120). Then make a diorama showing your animal in its natural habitat.

## What You Need

Mini-Critter Patterns (pages 116–119)
reference materials
Critter Information sheet (page 120)
pencil and eraser
markers and crayons
colored construction paper
stiff, thick black thread
scissors
glue
tape
clear plastic wrap
shoe box, gift box, or other similar box (lid not needed)
small twigs, pebbles, shells, cones, dry leaves, seed pods, etc.

## What You Do

1. Choose a critter from the patterns. Learn about where it lives. Using construction paper, create a background scene for your diorama. Glue it inside your box.

2. Decide how many critters you want in your diorama. Does your animal usually live alone, or with others of its kind?

3. Use the patterns to make your critters. Color them and cut them out. If you want to make them stiffer, glue them to construction paper and cut around them. You may wish to add legs or feelers made from black thread.

# Mini-Menagerie
## continued

4.  Create a natural-looking scene in your box, using the twigs, rocks, etc., that you have collected. You can make leaves from colored paper, or a branch from a cardboard tube. Try adding artificial flowers for the butterflies or clean fast-food trash for the flies and cockroaches.

5.  Arrange your critters among the scenery. Flying animals can be hung from threads or mounted on pins.

6.  Glue everything securely in place.

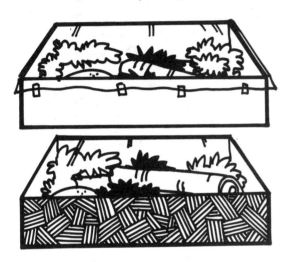

7.  Cover the open side of your box with plastic wrap. Attach it with small pieces of tape, as shown, stretching it tightly.

8.  Now cover the outside of your box with the construction paper, attaching the paper with glue or tape.

9.  Make a sign for your diorama with the critter's name and your name. Attach it where it can be easily seen.

10. Together with your classmates, make a menagerie by displaying your dioramas and information sheets where many people can enjoy them.

# Mini-Critter Patterns

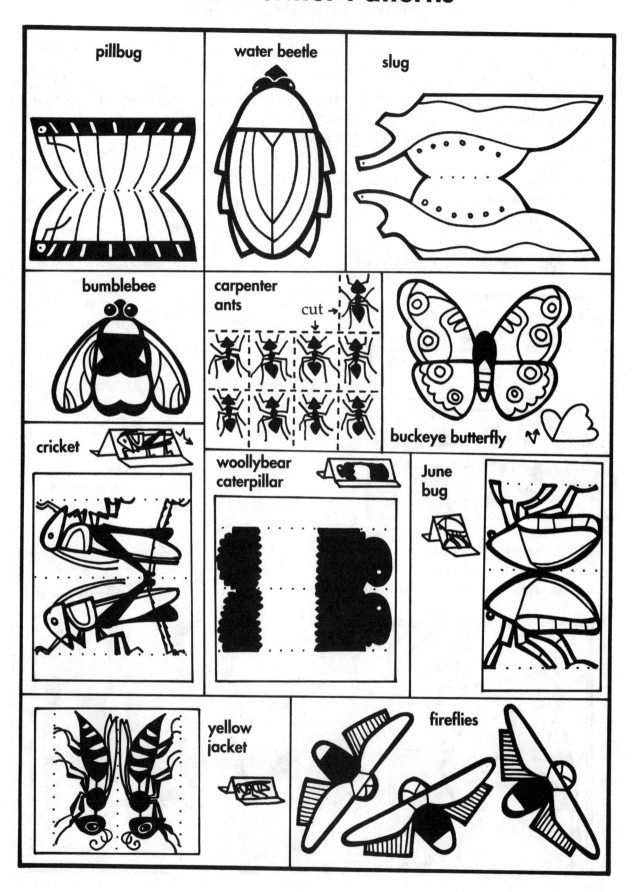

pillbug

water beetle

slug

bumblebee

carpenter ants

cut →

buckeye butterfly

cricket

woollybear caterpillar

June bug

yellow jacket

fireflies

# More Mini-Critters

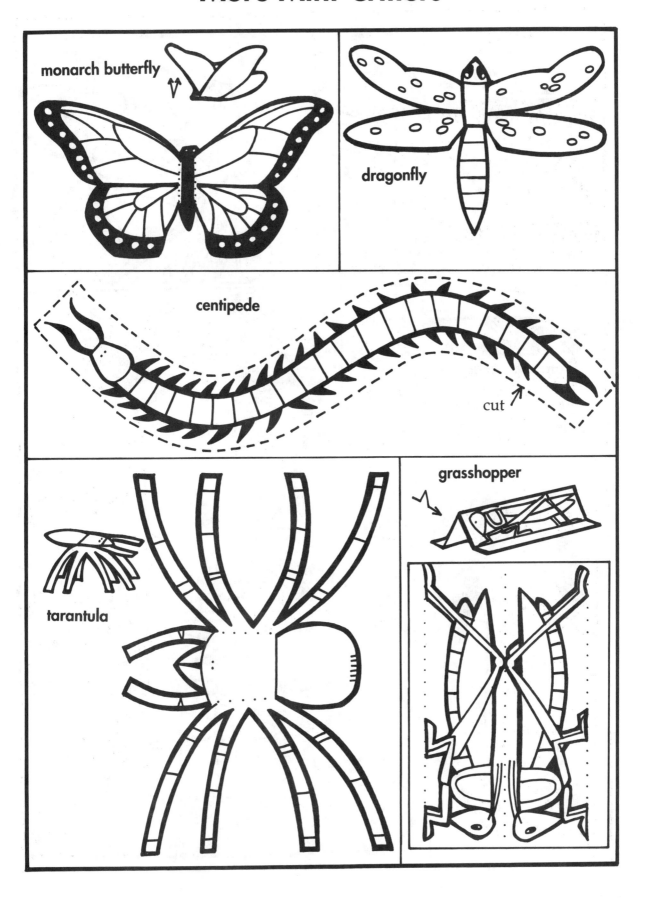

monarch butterfly

dragonfly

centipede

cut

tarantula

grasshopper

# More Mini-Critters

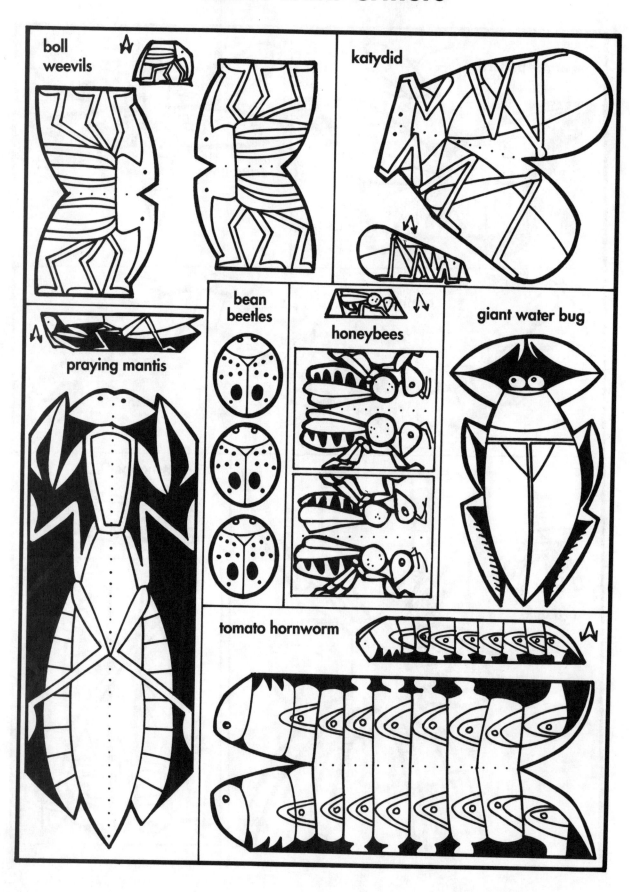

boll weevils

katydid

praying mantis

bean beetles

honeybees

giant water bug

tomato hornworm

# More Mini-Critters

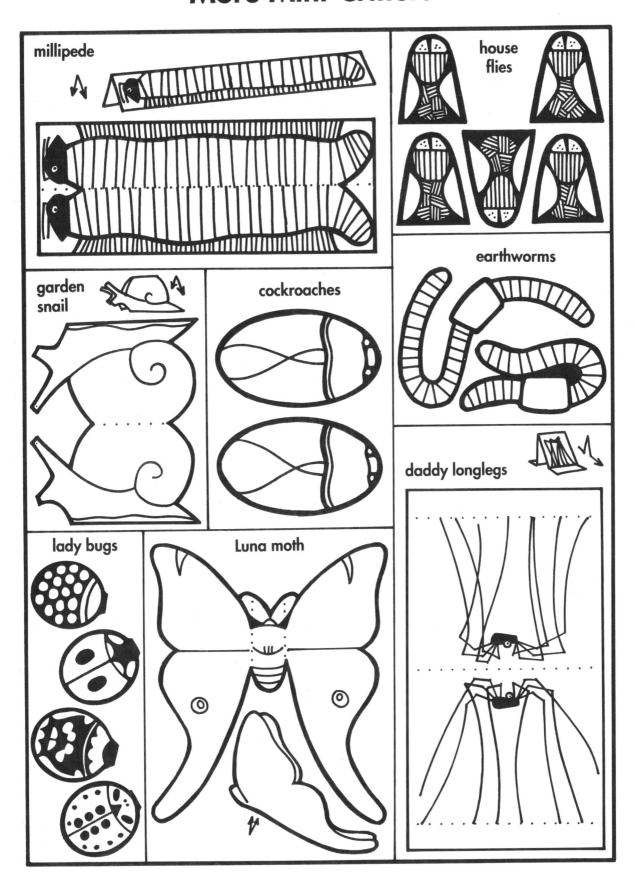

millipede

house flies

garden snail

cockroaches

earthworms

daddy longlegs

lady bugs

Luna moth

119

# Critter Information

Use resources such as books, magazines, and the Internet to learn about the animal you have chosen. If possible, observe your critter in the wild. Then answer these questions.

**Name of animal** _____

1. **Where does this animal live?**

   HOME: ☐ web  ☐ tree  ☐ nest  ☐ hole in the ground

   ☐ no special place  ☐ other _____

   HABITAT: ☐ desert  ☐ field  ☐ pond/stream  ☐ forest  ☐ park/yard

   ☐ inside a house  ☐ other _____

   IT USUALLY LIVES: ☐ alone  ☐ in a group of similar animals

2. **What does this animal eat?** _____

3. **Do other animals eat it?**  ☐ yes  ☐ no

   If so, which ones? _____

4. **How does this animal defend itself?**

   ☐ bites  ☐ stings  ☐ smells bad  ☐ tastes bad  ☐ looks scary

   ☐ runs/flies/hops away  ☐ hides  ☐ other_____

5. **How big does this animal get?** _____

6. **Does it lay eggs?**  ☐ yes  ☐ no

7. **How long does it live?**_____

8. **Is this animal mostly helpful or harmful to people?**

   ☐ mostly helpful  ☐ mostly harmful

   In what way(s)? _____